Abstract Resistance

FRANCIS BACON

LYNDA BENGLIS

ANTHONY CARO

SARAH CHARLESWORTH

BRUCE CONNER

WILLEM DE KOONING

LUCIO FONTANA

HOLLIS FRAMPTON

PHILIP GUSTON

RACHEL HARRISON

THOMAS HIRSCHHORN

ELLSWORTH KELLY

PAUL MCCARTHY

ROBERT MOTHERWELL

BRUCE NAUMAN

CADY NOLAND

CHARLES RAY

GEDI SIBONY

KARA WALKER

ANDRO WEKUA

CATHY WILKES

Published on the occasion of the exhibition Abstract Resistance, curated by Yasmil Raymond for the Walker Art Center.

Walker Art Center
Minneapolis, Minnesota
February 27–May 23, 2010

Abstract Resistance is made possible by generous support from Michael Peel, Lisa and Pat Denzer, Leni and David Moore, Jr., and the Robert Lehman Foundation. Curatorial research supported by Etant donnés: The French-American Fund for Contemporary Art. Cathy Wilkes' installation supported by the British Council.

The exhibition catalogue is made possible by the Andy Warhol Foundation for the Visual Arts and a grant from the Andrew W. Mellon Foundation in support of Walker Art Center publications.

Library of Congress Cataloging-in-Publication Data

Abstract resistance / [organized by Yasmil Raymond for the Walker Art Center]. -- 1st ed.
    p. cm.
  Published on the occasion of an exhibition held at the Walker Art Center. Minneapolis, Minn., Feb. 27-May 23, 2010.
  Includes bibliographical references.
  ISBN 978-0-935640-95-3 (pbk. : alk. paper)
  1. Art, Abstract--Exhibitions. I. Raymond, Yasmil. II. Walker Art Center.
  N6494.A2A227 2010
  709.04'052074776579--dc22

                              2010017087

First Edition ©2010 Walker Art Center

Every reasonable attempt has been made to identify owners of copyright. Errors or omissions will be corrected in subsequent editions.

Available through D.A.P./Distributed Art Publishers, 155 Sixth Avenue, New York, NY 10013
www.artbook.com

Design Director
Andrew Blauvelt

Publications Director
Lisa Middag

Designer
Dante Hong Carlos

Curatorial Assistant
Camille Washington

Editor
Karen Jacobson

Image Production
Greg Beckel

Translations
Michael Eldred

Proofreaders
Pamela Johnson, Kathleen McLean

Printed and bound in the United States by lulu.com.

cover, clockwise from left:
PHILIP GUSTON
Bombay 1976

RACHEL HARRISON
Huffy Howler 2004

ANDRO WEKUA
Spectator Standing 2005

THOMAS HIRSCHHORN
Abstract Resistance 2006 (detail)

Contents

Gedi Sibony

World of Isolated Lions

To occur is to relate. Aspects seek objects. Events are filtered directionally to demonstrate equivalencies.

(To articulate the conflict is to praise the availability of the state of life as mystery, accessible through simultaneous fields, while processing the need to portray things as such and its antithetical elements and doing it anyway to praise those too.)

A show happens in a place carefully crafted to accommodate versions of the experience of properties as they are engaged. Rooms are emptied and swept. Generally things are brought in, unpacked, placed, and met, ceremonially. There they subsist through night and day so that their effect has the opportunity to be transmitted and their cause to be ascertained. They are meant to persist beyond their proximity. The thing that happens can't be separated from any of the circumstances of the event.

The world is oblivious to not pinning itself down. How do you form an articulation of the world without bringing the world away from visibility? By eliminating the obscuring agents. The impulse of the act is a restoring of things with an accuracy toward the concise. The staging is continuous, and the reception is experienced as a passage. Points of transition greet supple generating beings asked to bear witness.

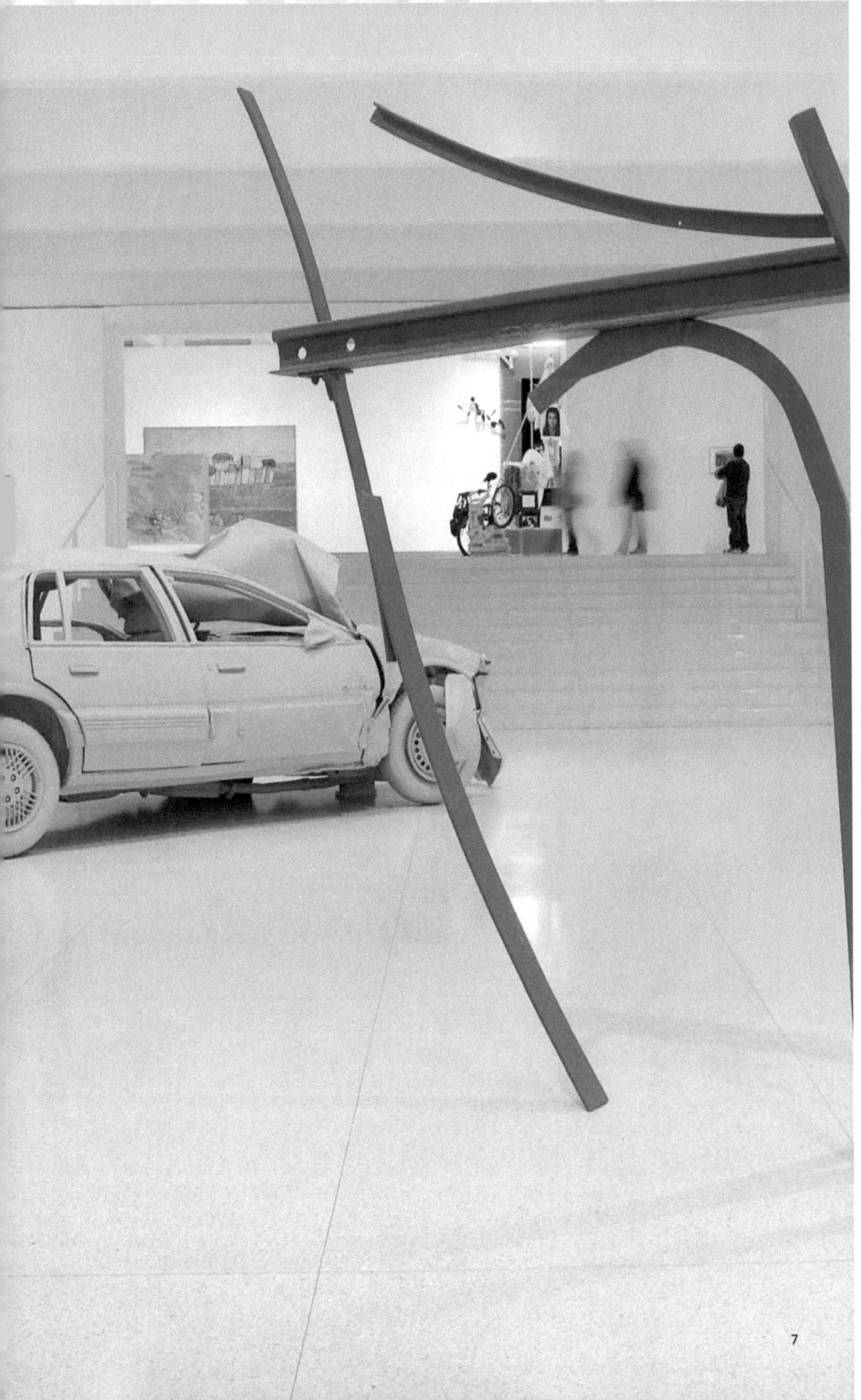

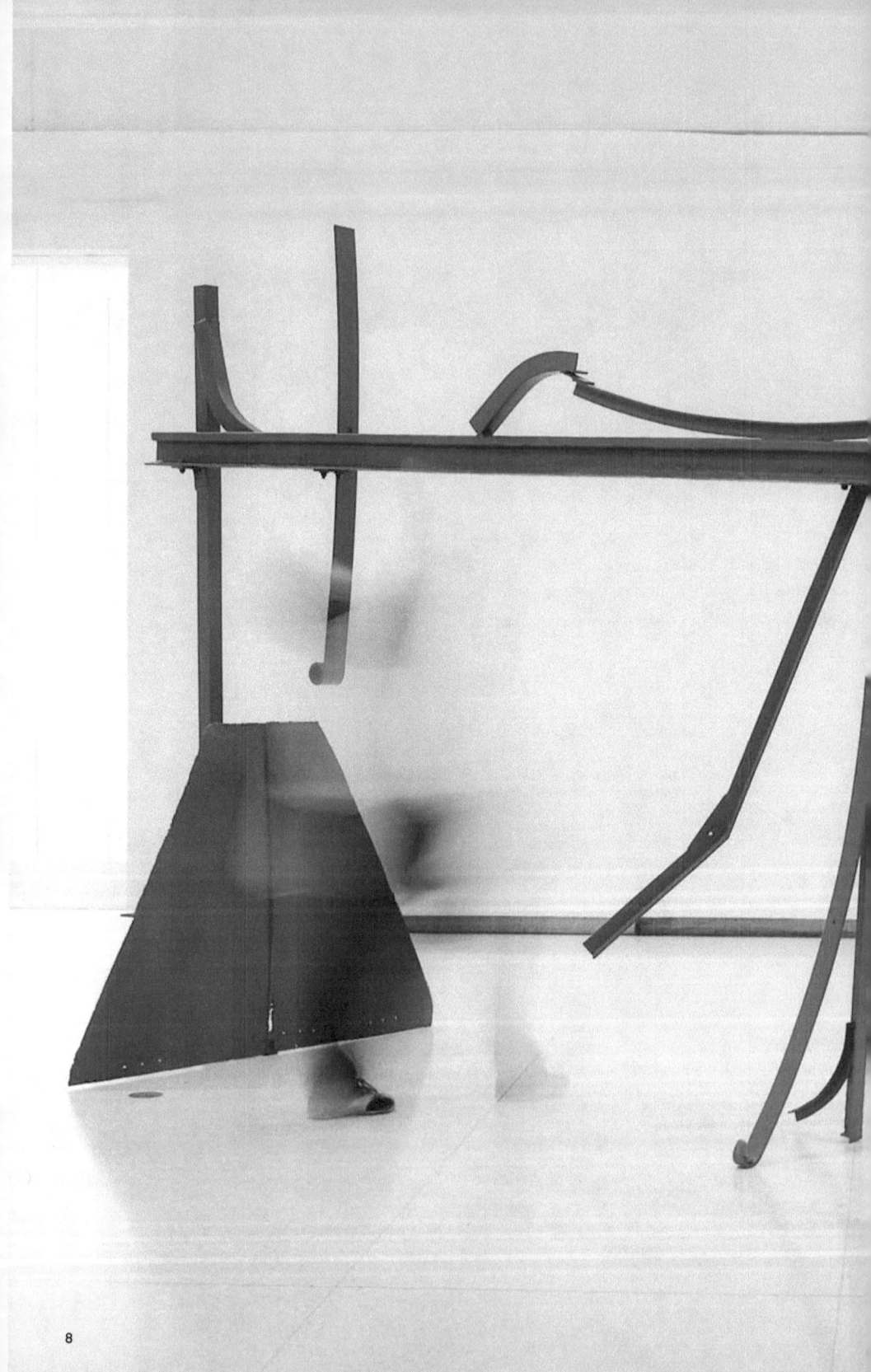

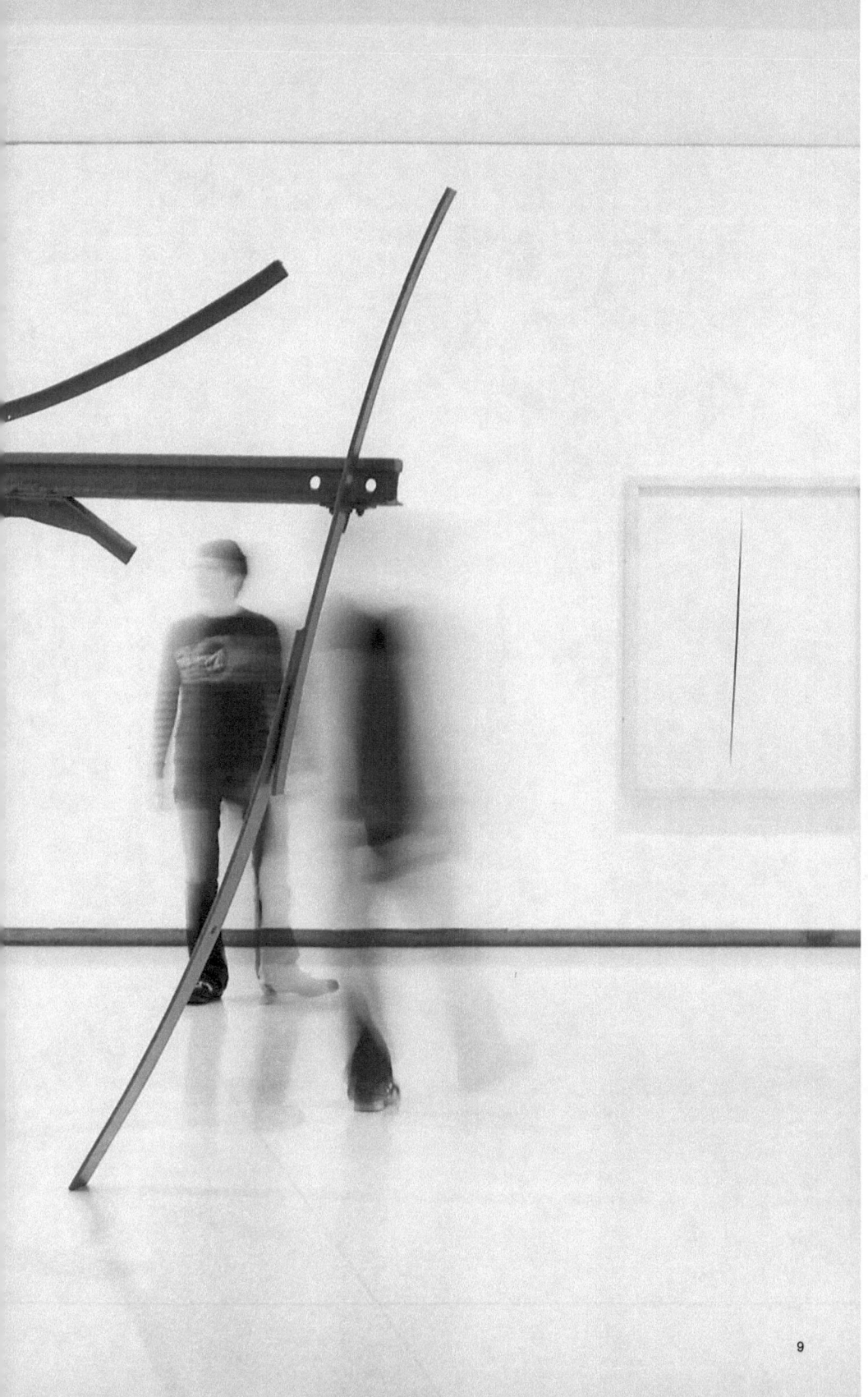

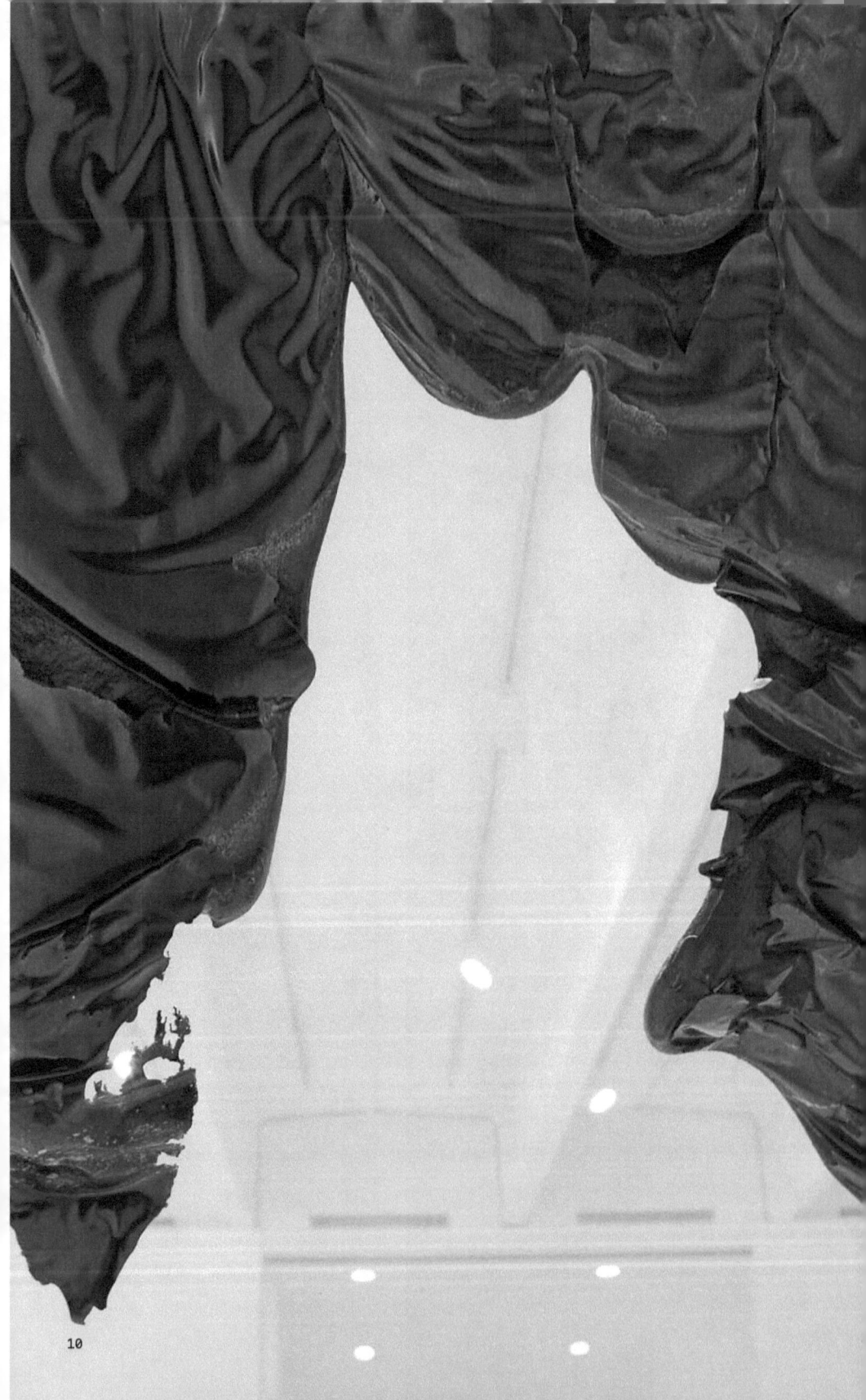

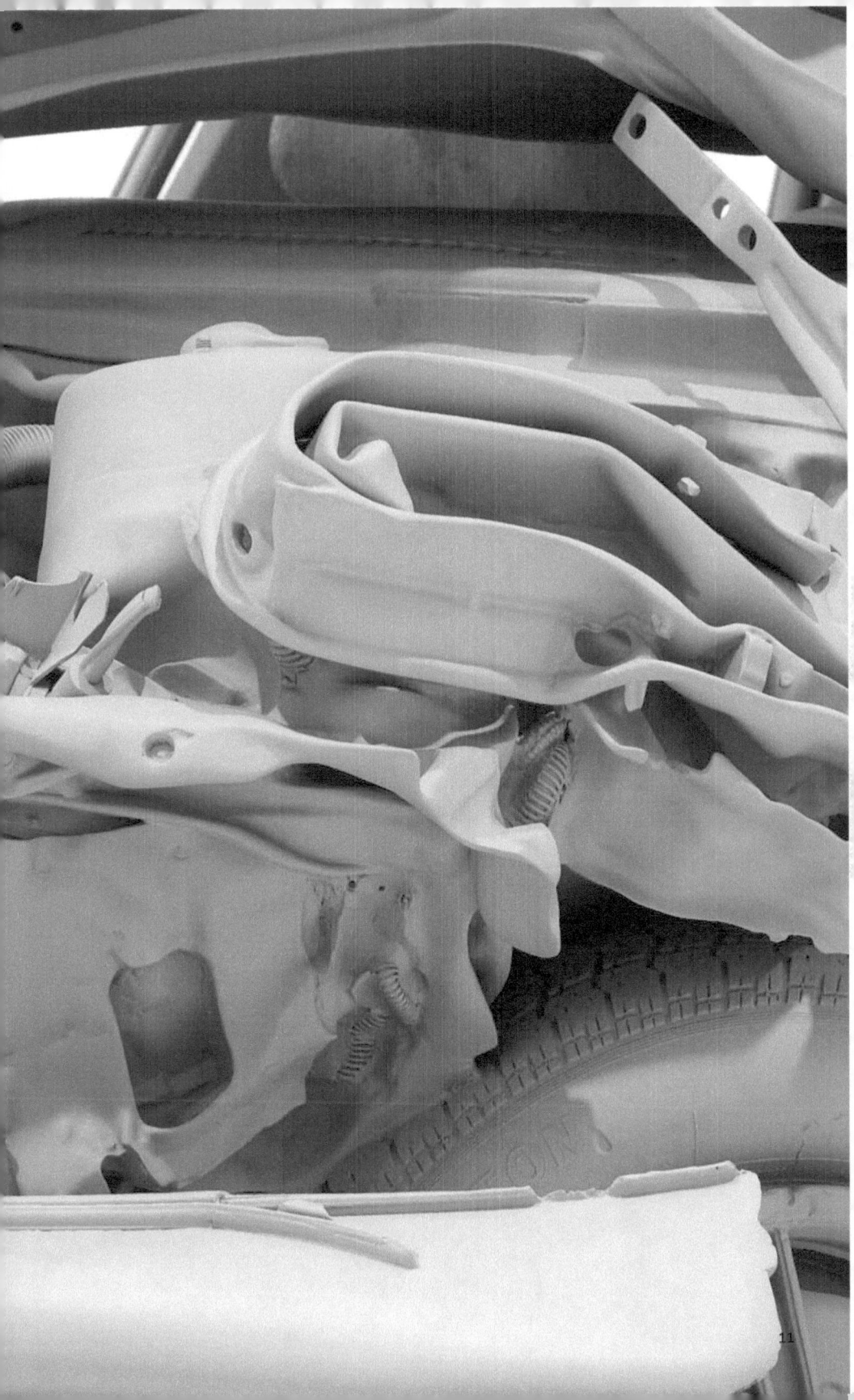

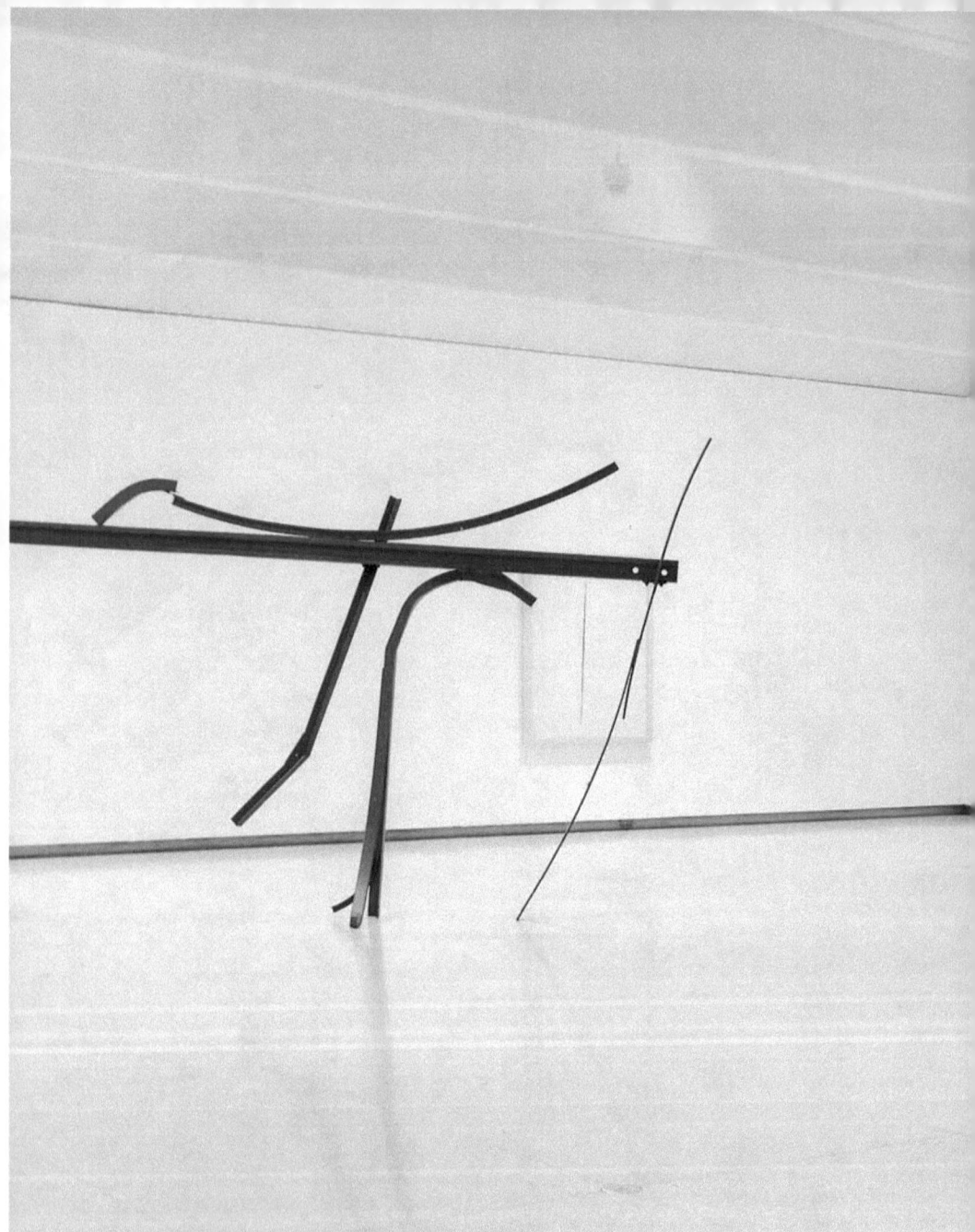

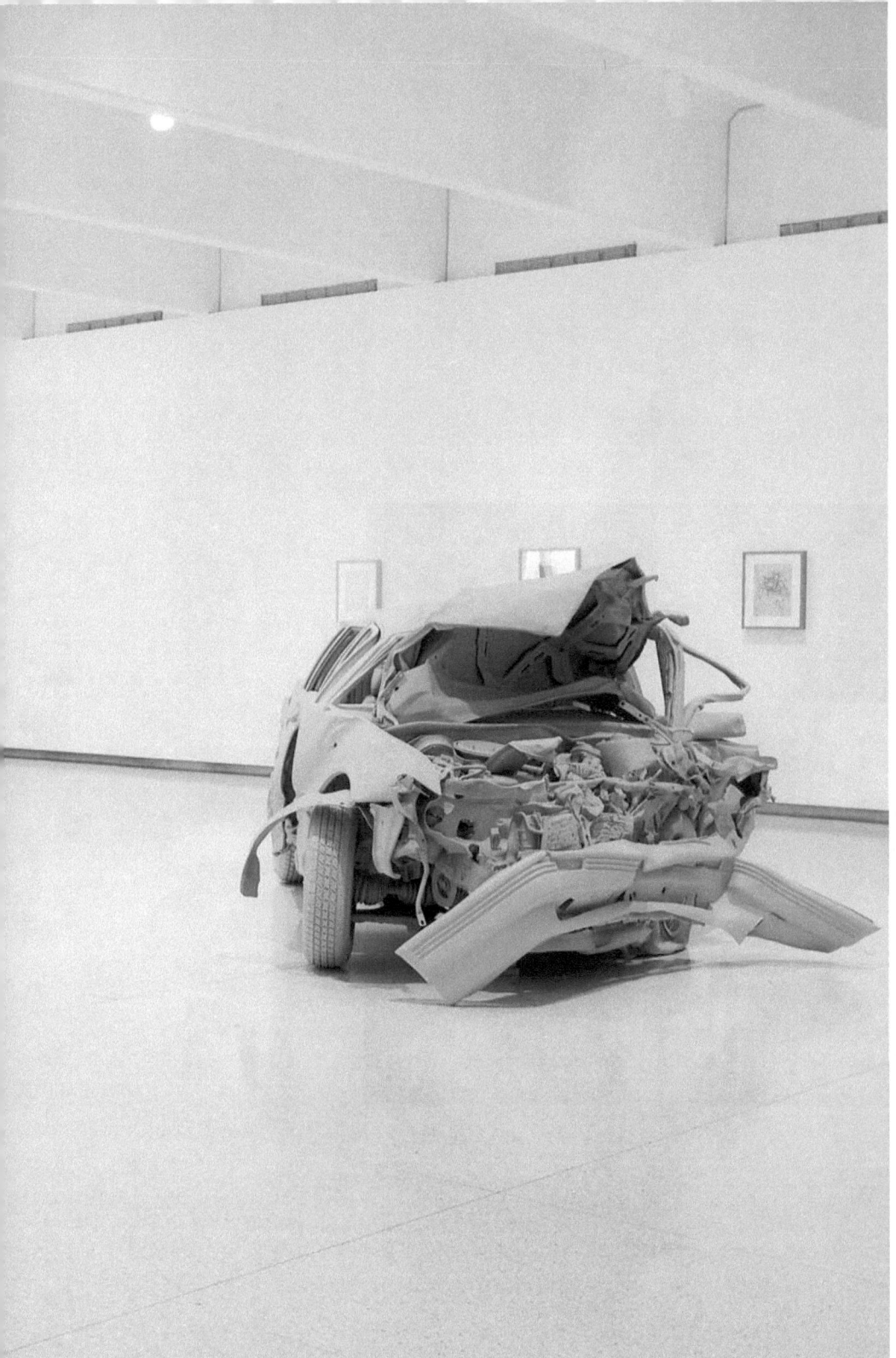

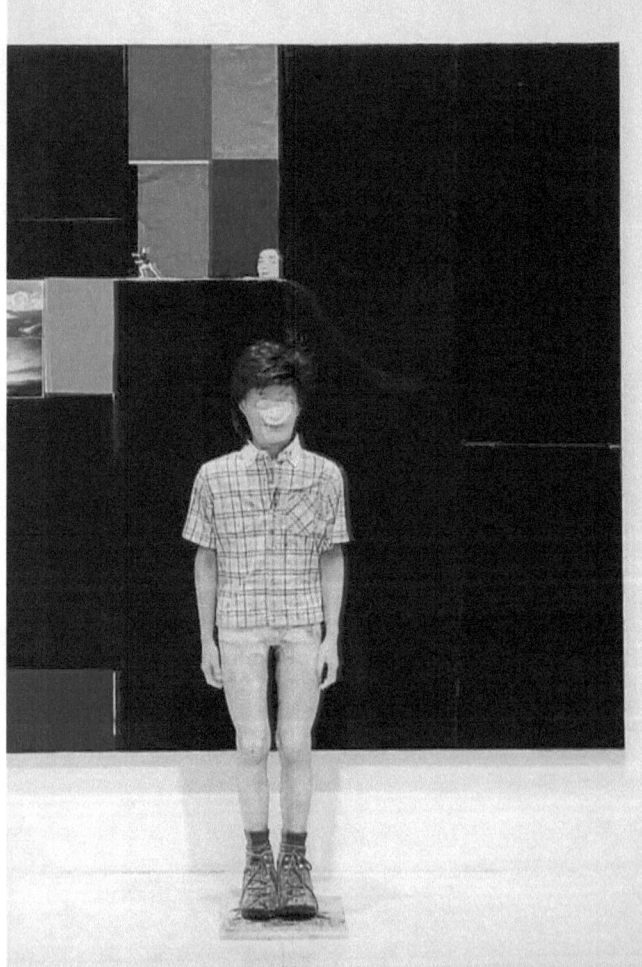

Yasmil Raymond

Contending with Comfort: The Possibility of an Abstract Resistance

In a review of Jean Daniel's book <u>L'ère des ruptures</u> (1979) titled "Pour une morale de l'inconfort" (For an Ethic of Discomfort), Michel Foucault recounts the story a Berlin journalist who asked several philosophers, including Immanuel Kant, in 1784, "What is Enlightenment?" Noting that it is debatable whether this question belongs to philosophy or journalism, he assigns a greater value to the journalist's question than to the philosopher's answers, admitting that fundamentally the newspaper reporter was asking the thinkers to rationalize a more difficult question: "What is it that has happened to us?" He added: "The concern to say what is happening...is not so much prompted by the desire to know always and everywhere what makes this happening possible but, rather, by the desire to make out what is concealed under that precise, floating, mysterious, utterly simple word 'today.'"[01]

As the first decade of the twenty-first century draws to a close, the notion of an ethical stance in contemporary art has regained immediacy and relevance. At a time when the barbarity of war "abstracts" hard truths, the creative process is informed by a heightened sense of critique accompanied by a refusal to seek political consensus. This criticality, which asserts its subjectivity despite its inability to take a moral position, is anarchic and seemingly distant from political reality. In contrast to the criticality of the avant-garde of the twentieth century, the contemporary approach to difference and the un-familiar is characterized by anxiety and vulnerability. For Foucault and others, the question of ethics rests in maintaining a level of discomfort with one's belief system, "never to con-sent to being completely comfortable with one's own presupposi-tions....To be very mindful that everything one perceives is evident only against a familiar and little-known horizon, that every certainty is sure only through the support of a ground that is always unexplored."[02]

On this amorphous ground, deliberately open to the possibil-ity of alienation, acts of resistance take new form. But what does it mean to equate the act of making art with resistance?

[01] Michel Foucault, "For an Ethic of Discomfort," in <u>Essential Works of Foucault, 1954–1984</u>, vol. 3, <u>Power</u>, ed. James D. Faubion (New York: New Press, 2000), 443.

[02] Ibid., 448.

To do so is to admit from the outset that the raison d'être of art is an aesthetic experience that carries critical substance; its necessity is to insist on the possibility of reaching a consensus with the beholder that brings about a collective agreement. But if the idea of consensus is abandoned, a criticality of difference emerges in which the work of art asserts its potentiality as an argument antagonistic to the persuasive rhetoric of political protest and propaganda. The notion of art as resistance is conceived not as a means to find answers, but as a basis for asking questions that might make it possible for us to face them. In this situation the encounter with the work of art unfolds a multitude of individual confrontations and contradictions. Art takes the form of a paradox, an apprehensive subject, simultaneously revealing information and resisting interpretation with subversive ambiguity and rebellious irreverence. The work of art, then, constructs a force field of tensions between what is revealed and what is withheld, between what lures and stuns us and what we permit to confront us. It is this interplay that sustains the resistance on both ends. In attributing critical value to the experience of art, we must refrain from reducing art to mere discussions of aesthetic programs and conceptual intentionality and instead consider discomforting positions and enigmatic declarations that challenge the reception and understanding of the work of art.

Historically works of art that withhold explanation have been associated with the notion of abstraction. Yet abstraction and all its histories center on a formal analysis that assumes that the meaning of the work is in the expression of its maker. Considering abstraction through the lens of "resistance" lends itself to an anachronistic approach to works of art that have responded to a historical context. In art, the critique of the existing world presents itself in the redemptive promise of an unfamiliar truth in which the very question of ethics is contingent on the presence of discomfort. As Theodor W. Adorno put it, "True injustice is always to be found at the precise point where you put yourself in the right and other people in the wrong."[03] From this point of view, an abstract resistance, in the broader sense, is the work of art that refuses an idealist narrative of normality while confronting the commodity of

[03] Theodor W. Adorno, quoted in Judith Butler, Giving an Account of Oneself: A Critique of Ethical Violence (New York: Fordham University Press, 2005), 61.

[04] Abstract Resistance is the title of a sculpture by Thomas Hirschhorn, one of four works—along with Chromatic Fire, Spatial Front, and Concrete Shock—included in his solo exhibition Superficial Engagement at Gladstone Gallery, New York, from January 14 to February 11, 2006. The encouragement and attention offered

by Thomas Hirschhorn from our first conversation about this exhibition has been extraordinarily important to me.

[05] Thomas Hirschhorn, letter to Sabine Windlin, published as part of Windlin's article "Beim Staatsfeind No. 1," Das Magazin, no. 17 (April 29–May 5, 2009): 37–40; translated for the present volume by Michael Eldred (72–79).

[06] Thomas Hirschhorn, "Superficial Engagement," artist's statement, Aubervilliers, October 11, 2005.

comfort with a barricade of contradictions and irreverence.[04]

The notion of an "abstract resistance" originates in the title of a work by Thomas Hirschhorn, a walk-in sculpture in the form of two platforms on which found images are displayed. These images include reproductions of images of bodies mangled and dismembered in bombings alongside reproductions of "healing pictures" and nail sculptures. In a statement published else-where in this publication, Hirschhorn described his reasons for juxtaposing this incommensurable imagery:

> In my work I show photos—some enlarged by photocopying—of exploded, dismembered, destroyed human bodies. My concern was not to show dead people but to show the absurd destruction of human bodies from Afghanistan, Iraq, 9/11, London suicide bombers, Bali, Israel, etc. We do know what that looks like! On websites we can see the latest images every day. It is no longer about killing, about death; it is about destruction. For me, the image of a mangled victim of a bomb attack or the image of a suicide bomber reaches a degree of abstraction way beyond what we can conceive with our imagination. I wanted to confront this degree of abstraction with the degree of abstraction of Art, of abstract Art. I wanted the different connections on the surface to confront one another.[05]

Hirschhorn's Abstract Resistance (2006) reintroduces an unfinished debate over the long-standing modernist distinction between abstraction and representation as irreconcilable pos-tures. The use of images of the bodies of war victims, or what the artist has called "bodies in abstraction," draws a parallel between abstraction's reductive nature and the ungraspable reality of war.[06] In this account of violence, which insists on acknowledging present-day atrocities through the act of looking, Hirschhorn's display of "abstraction" by way of found images provokes an experience of empathy that is ethically questionable in its excessiveness and political incorrectness. Constructed as a cul-de-sac in the corner of the gallery, the sculpture consists of two adjacent raised platforms. On one wall an "oriental" car-pet hangs alongside a banner that reads "Abstract Resistance," and underneath rests a plethora of cardboard and plywood panels and poster-size color printouts of snapshots of dead bodies. On the platforms are several freestanding structures made from tree trunks covered with nails and screws in the fashion of Vienna's Stock-im-Eisen, in which, urban legend holds, locksmiths will hammer a nail for good luck. Carefully placed in geometric modules and hanging mobiles is a second group of color reproduc-tions; this printed matter—culled from books, magazines, and the Internet—includes photocopies of Congolese nkisi nkondi, or nail figures, accompanied by reproductions of Emma Kunz's geo-metric "healing" pictures.

A triangular conflation of forces moves from the Kunz energy vectors to the medicinal powers of the African figures to the

17

violently mauled bodies.[07] Here the "bodies in abstraction" impose a psychological and physical effect that is as explosive as the actions depicted. Hirschhorn's Pandora's box holds no hierarchies of differentiation between abstraction and representation, craftsmanship and art, empathy and responsibility. Instead, each of these elements is encoded with shared meaning, each soiled with the obscenity of war and the material reality of the human body. Hirschhorn's work has addressed the creative process from a position of disobedience against interpretation and moral claim. His work situates art in the space of ethical discomfort. As disturbing as the subject matter of Abstract Resistance is, the very title in the hanging banner alludes to paradoxes between what seems to be the ineffectiveness of public denunciations and protest culture in the face of anarchic armed violence. The "abstract bodies" on Hirschhorn's platforms, to paraphrase the Italian filmmaker and writer Pier Paolo Pasolini, "oppose only with the violence of reason," revealing what intransigent militancy looks like, what destruction looks like. [08] Hirschhorn's antiaesthetic stance situates the work of art not as a cathartic experience but as a thinking experience that extracts reason from the abstraction that envelops it.

A similar resistance toward legibility is present in Philip Guston's late work. Guston, an artist who worked in varying degrees of abstraction throughout his career, continued to interrogate representation with a heightened awareness of the distorting apparatus of familiarity and the comfort of recognition. Judging from his pictures as well as his statements, Guston's concerns with the fate of humanity assumed a central position in his work from the outset. Whatever degree of skepticism underlined his thinking, his conception of art was qualified as an ethical problem, as formulated in one of his Poem-Pictures, with a text written by his wife, Musa McKim: "I thought I'd never write anything down again. Then I put on my cold wristwatch."[09] Can we speak of an abstract resistance as an articulation of courage to be willing to confront discomforting truths? Take, for example, Guston's Bombay from 1977, a field of collapsed horizons in which a band of gray paint across the bottom of the canvas functions as the ledge from which a pair of disembodied eyeballs look up across a landscape. These creatures from Guston's well-known repertoire are transformed into curious spectators who in their desire to "know more" actively point to a wasteland of collapsing clusters of pink forms topped with hobnailed shoes in the background. One the one hand, Guston precludes recognition by piling forms on top of one another with a degree of abstraction closer to Hirschhorn's distorted bodies. On the other hand, the fixed gaze of the eyeballs in the foreground conveys a different problematic, one of closeness.

Guston's Bombay is a picture of someone else looking into the thick of acrid truths. When he wrote, "the visible world, I think, is abstract and mysterious enough; I don't think one

needs to depart from it in order to make art," he implicitly
admitted to the exceptional ability of the work of art to acknowledge the illegibility of reality.[10] It is this abstracting
phenomenon, however, the complex interplay between seeing and
not seeing, that allows for the perception of profound truths
that cannot be easily grasped otherwise. Thus these "abstractions" are played out not only in formal terms but also in the
discrepancy between closeness and distance, knowing and not
knowing. One can see why Susan Sontag, in her work on interpretation, argued: "All works of art are founded on a certain
distance from the lived reality which is presented. This 'distance' is, by definition, inhuman or impersonal to a certain
degree; for in order to appear to us as art, the work must
restrict sentimental intervention and emotional participation,
which are functions of 'closeness.'"[11] In denying this objective distance, Guston brings "closer" the abstract nature of
violence, not to represent it, but to posit this concept outside
the realm of victims and perpetrators and emphasize its universal
implications. This drive, in a similar fashion to Hirschhorn's
bodies in abstraction, elicits uneasiness through the process of
self-recognition, as the anonymous victim is transformed into
our mirror image.

As in the works by Guston and Hirschhorn, proximity is a
major aspect of the relationship between the object and the
viewer in Charles Ray's Unpainted Sculpture (1997), a fiberglass
cast of more than one hundred individual parts of a wrecked
Pontiac Grand Am that was reassembled to its original scale and
painted matte gray. Unlike the former examples, Ray's hyper-
realist reproduction and neutral surfaces produce "closeness"
through the voyeurism of disbelief. We are thus not dealing
with the undignified violence of the human body. Rather, what
is at issue in Ray's cast of twisted parts and flat front tire
is the wreckage of a catastrophe, a conceptual abstraction. The
accuracy of Ray's man-made replica, which combines perfection
and perversity, brings about a second collision in the form of
repulsion. In other words, the act of looking at each detail—
from the open door of the glove compartment to the texture of
the seats to the allover mess of the front end—assumes ethical implications as the inspection of the surfaces narrows the
distance from the original disaster. But what appears to be an
aesthetic decision is actually a conceptual structure, as the
artist has acknowledged: "In contemporary art, surface is an

[07] Hirschhorn, letter to Sabine
     Windlin (see note 5).
[08] Pier Paolo Pasolini, "I Work
     All Day," in Roman Poems (San
     Francisco: City Lights, 2005), 87.
[09] Philip Guston, Poem-Pictures
     (Andover, Mass.: Addison Gallery of
     American Art, 1994), 71.
[10] Philip Guston, "Philip Guston
     Talking," in Theories and Documents

of Contemporary Art: A Sourcebook
of Artists' Writings, ed. Kristine
Stiles and Peter Selz (Berkeley
and Los Angeles: University of
California Press, 1996), 250
[11] Susan Sontag, "On Style," in Against
Interpretation and Other Essays
(New York: Picador, 1966), 30.

expression of anxiety, and no one is as anxious about surface
as I am."[12] Whereas the range of images in Hirschhorn's collage
denotes the excess and chaos of war, Ray's muted surfaces are
imbued with an inexpressive complicity stripped of anecdotal
facts but not of the interrogation of the sensorial experience.
"What's hard is to get the work to sit right," explains Ray
about his process, "to get the syntax of a piece exactly, as
Anthony Caro would say. It's a squishy, vibrant equation—
something when all the parts intersect perfectly, something
that breathes psychologically."[13]

In Unpainted Sculpture, it is the gray paint that inverts
the surface into an abstract concept, transforming the carcass
of the quintessential commodity of middle-class aspiration into
a motionless repository of violence. Ray's version of the disaster, reproduced in a monochromatic fiberglass mold, assumes the
aura of an industrial prototype of an oversize toy, ready for
its paint job. Resting on the floor, an iconic car model for a
generation of Americans is accorded the role of a different kind
of vessel, with its new associations of speed, mobility, expan-
sion, and catastrophe.

At first glance, the nature of an abstract resistance may
seem to echo the attitude of a conscientious objector, an
individual who tests single-handedly an accepted value of obedi-
ence. It is clear, however, that Hirschhorn's multipart collage,
Guston's obliterations, and Ray's cast are not simply objections
to conventions of art-making. What is striking about these works
is the artists' shared interest in doing something entirely different through a system of awkward decisions that resist decep-
tive explanations. Their works address the limitations inherent
in critique itself: the abstraction of ethics, the impossibility
of absolute agreement and understanding. At the same time the
articulation of such deceptions and contradictions in order
to destabilize the tyranny of comfort is characteristic of the
resistance. Several artists working today have explored these
concerns in relationship to the deterioration of the image and
have resorted to language for completion, presenting a different
variation on the idea of withholding and confronting through
a push-pull between the transmission of words and the visualiza-
tion of images. In an attempt to unpack meaning from language,
to make words speak to us, we do not "read" them in the traditional sense, but instead we imagine them as images and scenes.

The transference from reader to image-maker is the defensive
strategy employed in Kara Walker's series of ink drawings titled
Search for ideas supporting the Black Man as a work of Modern

[12] Charles Ray, quoted in Robert Storr, "Anxious Spaces," Art in America 86 (November 1998): 106

[13] Charles Ray, quoted in Steven Henry Madoff, "Art: The Animated Mind behind the Mannequin," New York Times, May 31, 1998, sec. 2.

[14] Kara Walker, Kara Walker: Bureau of Refugees (Milan: Edizioni Charta, 2008), 7.

[15] Francis Bacon, quoted in David Plante, "Bacon's Instinct," New Yorker, November 1, 1993, 93.

Art/Contemporary Painting. A death without end: an appreciation of the Creative Spirit of Lynch Mobs— (2007). Fifty-two statements, handwritten with sumi-e ink and brush on pieces of white paper the size of message boards or placards, are installed in a grid of four rows in what becomes a wall of sorrows. Each panel is handwritten in a different style, in a particular tone of voice and pace, so that they maintain an individual expressive character, visually acting out the tone of the utterance. Skin and blood are frequently mentioned, generally with no hint of self-righteous judgment, but often with the delusional pride of a skilled dominatrix with a wry and self-deprecating sense of humor. Fifty-two accounts, fifty-two disturbing confessions: the language deployed is reductive and straightforward as it raises questions of domination on all levels of human relationships, whether sexual, racial, social, or emotional. In every statement the artist in her adopted persona launches a verbal attack, as she admits, "that exposes, denies or conflates the language of the perpetrator with that of the victim." Furthermore, she adds: "None of these texts is restricted to the black body, necessarily, although that is my primary point of reference. Mostly they reflect the news of the moment, they fetishize the body in peril, and the perverse glee that can be had in making art out of history."[14]

The overall effect of reading through these accounts of merciless disfigurations of male and female bodies is not limited to the act of reading but spills into the realm of the imagination, our ability to improvise and conjure scenarios to serve as backdrops to the scripts. On reflection, the abstract dimension of Walker's bluntness is twofold. On the one hand, there is the brevity of the sentences, emptied of excessive adjectives, suggesting hysterical ranting. Deliberately adopting the non sequitur, she abruptly disrupts her own narrations, departing from the predictability of the cliché and displacing logic with outrageous speech of profound intensity and vulnerability. On the other hand, Walker's grid reveals another level of abstraction, in this instance the quintessential reductive composition of the Minimalist generation. In this instance, the accumulation of rectangles amasses into an expansive grid that breaks down the possibility of taking in the image in its entirety. Instead, the eyes must choose and focus on a particular statement, collapsing the geometric symmetry proposed by the grid with the excessive figurative language of the text.

Walker's work, no less than Hirschhorn's or Ray's, has centered on examining the creative process from a position of disobedience toward moral claims. The works of all three artists equate art with a debate in which the confrontation of what Francis Bacon repeatedly called the "brutality of facts" occurs only through an unconditional acceptance of contradictions that eschews utopian aspirations toward resolution.[15] Rather, their work embraces a concept of art as power relations in which the traditional role of the spectator is interrogated and constantly redefined.

In contrast to Walker's abundance of language, Sarah Charlesworth's April 21, 1978 from Modern History (1978), a series of forty-five black-and-white prints, constructs a different kind of abstraction through the subtraction of language. For Charlesworth, as for Walker, the abstracting nature of language as a way of constructing images allows us to decipher the signifying character embedded in them. This subgroup of the Modern History series focuses on the circulation of one particular image, a photograph of Italian prime minister Aldo Moro (1916–1978) released to the press by his kidnappers, the Brigate rosse (Red Brigades), which shows a poised Moro sitting in front of a banner with the name and insignia of the organization while holding a copy of the newspaper La Repubblica from April 19 whose headline reads, "Moro assassinato?" (Moro killed?).[16] The work consists of a row of black-and-white photographic reproductions of the front pages of forty-five international newspapers showing this image. With great precision and without altering the original format of the newspapers, Charlesworth masked the articles and image captions, replacing text with blank columns and leaving behind only the mastheads and the pictures. The real point of the work is not the actual event but the photograph itself, its use value and repetition as much as its testimonial nature. "Newspaper within a newspaper within a newspaper" is how the artist has described the recursive presence of the medium, which creates a type of mise en abyme.[17]

The use of the newspaper as a date marker to provide evidence of Moro's existence and refute the rumors of his death goes to the heart of the paradox of photography's loss of truth function and admits its new role as simulated reality. As Jean Baudrillard stated: "Of the same order as the impossibility of rediscovering an absolute level of the real, is the impossibility of staging an illusion. Illusion is no longer possible, because the real is no longer possible."[18] Are Charlesworth's front-page abstractions objectified violence for a global arena prepared to

[16] Moro would be killed two weeks later, on May 9.
[17] Sarah Charlesworth Studio, "Series: Modern History," http://www.sarahcharlesworth.net/series-view.php?album_id=34&subalbum_id=56.
[18] Jean Baudrillard, Simulations, trans. Paul Foss, Paul Patton, and Philip Beitchman (New York: Semiotext[e], 1983), 38.
[19] Ellsworth Kelly, "Notes of 1969," in Stiles and Selz, Theories and Documents.
[20] Ellsworth Kelly, quoted in Herbert Muschamp, "Critic's Notebook; One Vision: A Hill of Green at Ground Zero," New York Times, September 11, 2003.

[21] In an interview with Peter Gidal on May 24, 1972, in London, Frampton explained the meaning of the Greek term Hapax Legomena: "It means 'said one time.' Things said once. It refers to words that are found but once in the entire corpus of a literature. Sometimes they are found just once in the entire body of work of a poet. In some languages this amounts to a very large class" (Gidal, "Interview with Hollis Frampton," October 35 [Spring 1985]: 103).

consume it? In her resistance to providing a definitive answer, she reverses the effect, both formally and conceptually, trading verbal language for visual repetition, effectively taking advantage of photography's disengagement from questions of factuality and uniqueness in exchange for the speech power of abstracted latency.

Disappointed by the selection proceedings for a World Trade Center Memorial, on September 3, 2003, Ellsworth Kelly sent an unsolicited proposal to the late architecture critic Herbert Muschamp of the New York Times with a note. The sketch, titled Ground Zero (2003), is a trapezoidal piece of green paper glued on a newspaper clipping showing an aerial shot of the site. With its unassuming use of geometry, Kelly's proposition—to consider a flat field of color to occupy center stage, optically and spatially—attests to his long interest in taking inspiration from sites and objects and finding spatial solutions that orient the experience toward a relationship with emotions. Real space, a ground to regenerate and to take up the question of democracy anew, is a form of "ground zero" that Kelly recognizes is neces- sary to establish the context for reconciliation and tolerance. As the artist has observed, "Making art has first of all to do with honesty. My first lesson was to see objectively, to erase all 'meaning' of the thing seen. Then only could the real mean- ing of it be understood and felt."[19]

The formal implosion of Kelly's modest revelation imposes its presence through a carefully crafted absence. Clearly there is more than one way to fill the void. For some, building a he- roic monument, an emblem of uprightness and pride, would seem to perpetuate the intolerance that led to the attacks in the first place. Kelly's engagement implied exactly the opposite. As he wrote in the note accompanying his proposition: "I feel strongly that what is needed is a 'visual experience,' not additional buildings, a museum, a list of names or proposals for a freedom monument. These are distractions from a spiritual vision for the site: a vision for the future."[20] Apparently simple, Kelly's proposal consists of a perceptual event, lacking any element of propaganda but simply putting forth the daring idea of an unob- structed space in which to conceive tangible realities. It is important to recognize the interplay between erasing and remem- bering, as the two forces emanate from the same authorial space.

Hollis Frampton is another artist whose work focuses our attention on a nonlinear correspondence between words and im- ages in order to access the inner world of his imagination and memory. In (nostalgia) (1971), the first film in the seven-part series Hapax Legomena (1973), he resorted to the plasticity of time and speech to construct a narrative of anticipation and in- conclusive abstractions.[21] Choosing thirteen photographs he made between 1959 and 1966, Frampton proceeded to film the process of burning them on a hotplate, accompanying these visuals with a voice-over detailing anecdotal facts about the images. What we see, however, is not in synch with what we hear.[22] By way of using the anticipatory nature of the voice-over, Frampton constructs a split between image and anecdote, preventing them from reconciling in the present tense. Here movement and time, what I take to be the most evocative aspects of his filmic syntax, are intimately connected, forging a correspondence between the disappeared image and the narrator's voice. Narration precedes the fire.

In Frampton's hands, language consumes itself, devouring its own ability to recount past experiences and conjure memories. Turning away from narrative, the film depends on real time as a "special effect" that explicitly determines the film's form and structure, each scene framed by the duration of the melting photograph, encouraging us to complete the narrative ourselves. [23] The title (nostalgia), lowercased and enclosed in parentheses, speaks of Frampton's interest in the poetry of the term. As he has stated, "In Greek the word means 'the wounds of returning.' Nostalgia is not an emotion that is entertained; it is sustained. When Ulysses comes home, nostalgia is the lumps he takes, not the tremulous pleasures he derives from being home again."[24] The past keeps returning as each photograph disappears within the flames, and a different kind of preservation process occurs, one that gives access to a passage in time, this time as moving image surveying Frampton's artistic origins as photographer, his encounters with his surroundings, street scenes, his friends (Carl Andre, Larry Poons, James Rosenquist, Frank Stella, Michael Snow), and himself.

The parallel between erasure and absence that Frampton uses in his film conjures the absence of a face in the tension between individual and universal identity. The clandestine face, with its ability to deface and hide, is invoked in a two-part work by Andro Wekua. Spectator Standing (2005) consists of a life-size cast in beeswax of an androgynous child whose eyes have been covered with a thick coat of opaque white paint. Blinded by the heavy pigment, the spectator, as the figure is referred to in the title, is absorbed in his or her own thoughts, in a state of introspection. Hanging on the wall behind the figure is a large square canvas covered with a collage of multicolored felt pieces and found images from the artist's archive, including magazine clippings of tropical sunsets and idyllic landscapes. The figure faces the beholder, its back to the canvas, its blank gaze adding to the discomfiting effect of its genderless naked body. This motionless and blinded figure recalls the allegorical figure Justice, deprived of sight and thereby protected from subjectivity and bias.

[22] The voice-over script was narrated by Frampton's friend, the filmmaker Michael Snow.
[23] Gidal, "Interview with Hollis Frampton," 105.
[24] Bruce Jenkins and Susan Krane, Hollis Frampton: Recollections and Recreations (Cambridge, Mass.: MIT Press, 1984), 56.

In Wekua's two-part composition, as in Frampton's work, memory is bound up with the isolation and denial involved in a tenuous relationship with the past. Spectator Standing is the sole witness and inheritor of a blinding historical memory, a body altered from its identity, facing forward with a cautious distance. It is the paint smeared over the eyes that cancels the spectator's identity, accentuating the ambiguity of this balancing act between abstraction and figuration and between painting and sculpture to render a hybrid form that resists the spectator's direct gaze.

The main opponent of an abstract resistance is a unified narrative and characterization. In this regard the mythical figure Prometheus has symbolic resonance. We are told that Prometheus was bound to a rock as part of his punishment from Zeus for disobeying him by providing fire to humans. His plight involved coexisting with an inanimate object, which metaphorically became part of his body. Such a conflictual bond between forms is found in Rachel Harrison's Huffy Howler (2004), a freestanding sculpture in which found materials and images are combined with handmade forms. An assemblage of parts—a base, a bicycle, handbags, rocks, an extension pole, a sheepskin, and a photograph—the sculpture holds its tenuous balance through a calibrated puzzle of weight and lightness. The bicycle sits atop an amorphous base of randomly piled bricks with one pedal anchored in a niche between two bricks, the back wheel in midair, while the front one, with a flat tire, rests on the ground. Hanging from one of the handles is a cluster of black handbags filled with rocks, stones, and gravel. Extending from the back of the bicycle is a Mr. LongArm extension pole, strapped to the brakes with the help of a spool of wire. Hanging from the pole is a piece of sheepskin flagged with a photograph, a head shot of Mel Gibson as his character in the 1995 movie Braveheart.

The monochromatic podium, made from bricks and coats of purple Parex stucco, is difficult to ignore as it functions not only as the main foothold and source of equilibrium but also as a deliberate element of exuberance and wayward humor. Harrison's base treats matter and surface as idioms of poignant resonance. Color again, as in Ray's Unpainted Sculpture, is a patina to the degree that it efficiently seals the surface of the material underneath, abstracting its relationship to the whole. Given the directness of Harrison's choices, the selection of a Huffy Howler mountain bicycle seems far from random, alluding, if tangentially, to Gibson's haughty personality. This balance of formality and self-deprecating humor speaks to a relationship of materials to themselves, a self-examination that points to a critical reading that makes the search for meaning into an open-ended task, one that asserts resistance through its distance from final judgment.

A second freestanding sculpture by Harrison, Al Gore (2007), is a megalith of abstract eloquence, barricading the space with

its autonomous volume. Equally compelling is the painted surface
that camouflages in bright greens, oranges, pinks, and yellows
the coarse brushstrokes of white stucco. As with Huffy Howler,
the colors are lush, and the stucco resembles frozen buttercream
icing. One is compelled to circumambulate it to inspect the
shifting colors of its surface, and in the process one discovers
that one side of the sculpture is lighter than the other, as
if it has evaporated or melted away. A second element, a classic
round Honeywell thermostat, reminds us that the sculpture is
named after the protagonist of the 2006 documentary An Inconve-
nient Truth, former vice president and environmental activist
Al Gore. The thermostat is here not to measure the changes in
the temperature in the room but to contradict its function, presenting itself as a theoretical error, an obsolete oracle that
offers an utterly superfluous prediction of change.

In fact, Harrison's eclectic approach to constructing form
is evidence of her concern with the impossibilities and illegibility of a unified declaration of the message of the work.
By introducing contradictions, she models her own idiom of
struggle, insisting on expanding the logic of material choices
while concealing speculation. This is evident in Chicken (2008),
in which the construction of the plywood box that dominates the
work is smooth and even, sharply contrasting with the exterior
paint job, the brushstrokes infused with the stereotypical
splashes and scribbles of gestural painting. Nearly seven feet
long, the box sits on a short white pedestal a foot from the
floor, underscoring the ambiguity of its possible function.
Looking at it from afar, we realize that it is not a plinth but
that this sarcophaguslike box insists on being an autonomous
form, with its colorful painted surfaces, its open side, and
its rubber chicken toy sitting in a bed of sawdust. Like Al
Gore, this is a two-sided sculpture. Hanging from the back is
a framed photograph of a leftover plate of fried chicken. In
this instance, Harrison, who uses photography in her work in-
terchangeably with found objects and handmade forms, staggers a
threefold formal correspondence between the paint job, the image
of fried chicken, and the materiality of the rubber dog toy. Her
hermetic imagery and forms seem driven by contradictory desires
to undermine classification and simultaneously to evoke recognition. This aesthetic provocation, calculated in its abstract
conceptualization, mounts a resistance to the traditional role
of spectatorship of consumption of evidence, appealing for an
experience of art from a place where nothing is ever certain.
What is resistance, after all, if not this rigorous questioning
of false consensus?

The use of paint to physically obliterate surfaces—as
exemplified by the work of Ray, Wekua, and Harrison—operates
in a manner similar to the principle of deletion found in
Frampton's film and Charlesworth's photomontage. In these works
the disappearance of the image and of language explicitly leads

the beholder into a sensorial experience of uncertainty and
discomforting abstraction. Similarly, fragmented surfaces and
distorted images define this abstract resistance. The presence
of ruptures, cracked exteriors, and soiled surfaces is not the
result of desecration or defacement. On the contrary, these
forms are produced through accumulation and inflections of touch
and the application of materials to surfaces, channeling the
physicality of the human body in dialogue with the resulting
object or image.

This position is exemplified by the work of Cathy Wilkes,
who with a deep sense of precision has ventured to restore access to the innermost assertions of bodily presence. Her floor
piece Galilee (2009–2010) is a multipart environment that
invokes an archaeological site composed of recently unearthed
findings spread out for inspection and classification. The main
elements in the composition are two types of objects: those that
stand vertically and those that rest horizontally. Three glass
aquariums have been smeared with a thick coat of oatmeal por-
ridge that makes a muddy impasto on the surfaces. Placed inside
are various objects: toys, glass jars, and pieces of pottery.
Several cagelike forms made from tree branches stand nearby,
while a life-size figure of a knight dressed in armor rests on
the floor. "This work relates to infancy," admits the artist.
"Thinking of it as a beginning which isn't left behind but is
continuous and deep inside, which is the softness of a person
when they have experienced being not aware of their own separation from another, and experience something else, an almost
physical incompleteness or openness."[25] The viewer's proximity
to the objects demands careful movement and a sense of poise and
attention to the precariousness of their physical state. Each
element is a vessel, a carrier of other vulnerable emotions,
utterly fragile and charged with precision by the susceptible
presence of the artist's hands. This trove of childhood tokens,
dirtied bowls, and petrified residues of playtime is embedded
with codes of affection, touched surfaces, and premonitions of
motherly alliance and protection. Through a laborious method
of construction and alteration, Wilkes derives from objects,
without anthropomorphizing them, ideas of solitude, hunger, and
loss, written into the exhausted surfaces.

The concern with material associations finds a different
and more spatial dimension in Gedi Sibony's work. His multipart
installation, like Wilkes' scattered forms, unfolds into an
unassuming environment. Both artists share a process of accumulation and meticulous attention to salvaged materials. These
are not just found objects or art materials but functional items
commonly associated with construction sites and demolition—

[25] Cathy Wilkes, e-mail correspondence
    with the author, June 26, 2009.

drywall, cardboard, carpets, and plywood—and domestic set-
tings. For Sibony, materials are spatial and possess qualities
often lost in our daily experiences, which may allow us to move
beyond the use value ascribed to them and grant them discursive
power. Words in Sibony's work are primary material that together
with matter point to the integral role of assembling and into-
nation in the relationship of form and space. Uninhibited by
the precarious nature of modest materials, Sibony brings into
play an unassuming semantics of remnants and particles to return the beholder's attention to the realm of the senses. It is
difficult to consider Sibony's room-size installation without
speaking about the sensation of lightness, the poetry of weight
that hovers over each of the elements in the composition. At
the entrance the first image that catches our attention is the
blurred, spray-painted stencil of geometric forms, a grid of
circles and triangles that gives us the sense of a faint shadow.
The title of the wall piece is Than (2006-2007), a common word
that can function as a conjunction or a preposition to draw
comparisons between things, the perpetual pursuit of differentiation and subjectivity. Enacting a tangible comparison is a
second element sitting parallel to the wall, So (2007), which
consists of a freestanding structure made from three pieces of
plexiglass glued together in the form of an inverted U that
casts a shadow on the wall. Following this trail of reduced
forms, we encounter the centerpiece of the room, a cardboard
column that seeks a different kind of presence. Shhhh (2007)
is accompanied by a television monitor playing a ninety-minute
video of a still image of television static running on a loop,
which continues to change over time as the tape deteriorates. As
the onomatopoeia of its title suggests, the white flakes on the
screen acquire the role of a sandglass that measures the passing of time. Against a window, The World in Its Mouth (2007), a
silvery white piece of pegboard, filters light into the space
through its peepholes. A second wall piece, Not Too Different
(2006), reverses gravity, bringing into play the idea of an
elevated ground.

Similar to Wilkes' choices, which tend to be cautious and
diligent, Sibony's process is one of transference, spareness,
and displacement with a high degree of austerity when it comes
to construction. As the artist contends: "It became natural to
use things that are on hand, or materials that are light, available, and easy to move around. I like to gather the unused. To
use what I already have. Then I put them to work to serve something else."[26] In this instance, employing a carpet, a box of
cardboard, a sheet of pegboard, and plexiglass, he brings forms
and colors into dialogue with the space, noting the presence of
lights and shadows on the floor and walls, constructing permuta-
tions of subtle effects that respond to the changing light and
the speed of perception. Sibony reaches out to the most basic
28 forms to reveal two spaces happening at once, one where precari-

ous abstractions come about on the floor and walls, and a second that begins to take form through language.

Under the distress of discomforting truths, to insist on breaking the silence despite indifference and censorship remains a necessary, if not indispensable, concern of art. It is relevant to cite Adorno again as he made a declaration along the same lines: "The abundance of real suffering permits no forgetting; Pascal's theological 'On ne doit plus dormer' [Sleeping is no longer permitted] should be secularized. But that suffering—what Hegel called the awareness of affliction—also demands the continued existence of the very art it forbids; hardly anywhere else does suffering still find its own voice, a consolation that does not immediately betray it."[27] The strategy of an abstract resistance consists in a thought process that produces ruptures and cracks in the surface of the complacent mindset that attempts to normalize barbarity. Refusing to declare its intentions forthrightly, the work of art nevertheless states its urgent critique in the face of indifference, rejecting apathy and insisting on accountability.

Abstract resistance is an attitude that questions the privileges and fallacies of exactitude and proposes an experience of art as an experience of thought. Against the perilous status granted by Paul Virilio in his diagnosis that "art is the casualty of war," abstract resistance is characterized by a more complicated relationship with the exigencies of the task of confronting one's own dichotomies and assured certainties.[28] Perhaps more importantly, an abstract resistance requires indiscipline and refusal to compromise at the risk of rejection in order to have a relationship with the work of art within the given world, that is, the world of today. Thus to consider an "ethic of discomfort," as Foucault proposed three decades ago, demands that we abandon silence-inducing declarations in exchange for a "poke in the eye" that interrogates our sensibilities, scandalizes our senses, and awakens the experience of art from critical inertia.

[26] Philippe Vergne, "A Conversation with Gedi Sibony," in Gedi Sibony (Zurich: JRP/Ringier, 2009), 42.

[27] Theodor W. Adorno, Notes to Literature, trans. Shierry Weber Nicholsen, vol. 2 (New York: Columbia University Press, 1992), 88.

[28] Paul Virilio and Sylvère Lotringer, The Accident of Art (New York: Semiotext[e], 2005), 17.

Cathy Wilkes
Pay Attention

The title is disciplinarian, aggressive on a certain level.

It comes from Simone Weil's ideas about attention. Attention is concentration without thoughts, the disembodiment of a person to make space for God. Looking outward, I won't allow myself to observe, but rather I regard everything beyond my own emptiness as active agents that will make themselves known.

If this attention is the model, then we all are equal and have equal capacity; there is no one who is more sensitive than someone else. Signs of distance, shapes, and the geometric relations that become present in her make a symmetry and mediation with her cosmos and an equilibrium with the forces of nature. As a collection of considerations are not searched out, something comes forward slowly, folding and intimately pressing on top of itself. Rather than a clear presence, what form can it take?... Formalism and contemplation have to disappear: they're too active; they seem a violent form of production.

Attention has a softness, a register of incompleteness like a baby clinging to her mother, which seems to soften everything that is in relation to it. But even if it is such a gentleness, the thrill of attention is that it forces her, in some respects, to give up the vantage of life and to be able to die while living.

Marcus Steinweg

Nine Theses on Art

The definition of art that I attempt to give
in this essay culminates in the assertion that
art asserts a consistency owed to its opening
to inconsistency. We will see that the concept
of art, like that of the human subject, must
open up to non-art and the nonsubjective in
order to situate art and the subject, together
with all their claims to autonomy, on the line
of fracture between reality and ideality, the
possible and the impossible, the particular and
the universal.

The nine theses are:

1. Art is that which generates a concept
   of art.
2. The artwork implies a surpassing and
   transgressing of its factual conditions.
3. An artwork is something other than
   (merely) a document of its times.
4. Art articulates a difference from the
   texture of facts.
5. The artwork is the affirmation of
   this difference.
6. This affirmation takes place as an
   assertion of form.
7. Every assertion of form is indebted to
   making contact with formlessness.
8. Making contact with formlessness corresponds
   to making contact with truth.
9. Art's making contact with truth opens it
   up to universality.

1. Art is that which generates a concept of art.

"Art likewise is in no way simply equivalent with artworks, for artists are always also at work on art and not only on artworks."[01]

How can the interrelationship among these three concepts be defined: What is art? What are artworks? What is an artist? How do these concepts fit together? "Art stirs," Adorno says, "most energetically where it decomposes its subordinating concept."[02] The concept of art cannot be reduced to that of the artwork because every (authentic or real) artwork cannot be reduced to any preceding concept of art, but rather inaugurates a concept appropriate to itself. The work is never exhausted in exemplifying an established, officially sanctioned concept of art. What the work achieves divides into a resisting and an affirmative element. The work embodies resistance against the existing order, against art as an already weakened cultural production with diminished capacity to resist. There is an irreconcilable difference between art and culture, for which reason art is compelled to defend itself against culture and its imperatives. An artist is someone who brings forth a concept of art that did not exist before. Only those artworks count that, instead of inscribing themselves into an instituted concept of art, generate a concept opposed to the instituted concept. It is always a matter of opening up in the dynamics of production to a still undefined concept of art; it is never a matter of a routine program oriented toward fixed norms.

"In truth," Adorno says, artworks are "force fields in which the conflict is carried out between the commended norm and what is seeking expression in them. The higher they rank, the more energetically do they fight out this conflict, frequently renouncing affirmative success."[03] The artwork articulates the conflict between what exists and the new so that the work enters

[01] Theodor W. Adorno, "Toward a Theory of the Artwork," in Aesthetic Theory, ed. Gretel Adorno and Rolf Tiedemann, trans. Robert Hullot Kentor (Minneapolis: University of Minnesota Press, 1997), 182.
[02] Ibid.
[03] Theodor W. Adorno, Ohne Leitbild: Parva Aesthetica (Frankfurt am Main: Suhrkamp, 1967), 11. On the determination of the philosophical text and the artwork as a force field, see Adorno's theses from Zum Studium der Philosophie (1954): "Philosophical texts do not have any reified, fixed meanings but—in this regard similar to artworks—are force fields, in principle inexhaustible; the better one knows them, the more they give, and repeated reading is indispensable" (in Wolfram Schütte, ed., Adorno in Frankfurt: Ein Kaleidoskop mit Texten und Bildern [Frankfurt am Main: Suhrkamp, 2003], 226–31). The stimulus to view "the codified philosophies as force fields," Adorno says, came from Krakauer. Cf. Theodor W. Adorno, Noten zur Literatur III (Frankfurt am Main: Suhrkamp, 1965), 84.
[04] Theodor W. Adorno, "Society," in Aesthetic Theory, 238–39.
[05] Ibid., 238.
[06] Theodor W. Adorno, "Art, Society, Aesthetics," in Aesthetic Theory, 2.
[07] A form of unbounding but nevertheless a form. Because "form transcendence" is the form of the artwork, it remains threatened by what Adorno calls the "romantic principle" (characteristic in music, from which Adorno draws many of his examples, above all for Robert Schumann, but also for Gustav Mahler and Alban Berg): "the giving

as an arena for carrying out a differentiation (or difference) in which the established understanding of art meets an objection. At the same time it must remain clear that a distinct separation between the existing and new remains an unfulfillable challenge: "Even the category of the new, which in the artwork represents what has yet to exist and that whereby the work transcends the given, bears the scar of the very-same underneath the constant new. Consciousness, fettered to this day, has not gained mastery over the new, not even in the image: Consciousness dreams of the new but is not able to dream the new itself."[04] The artwork draws its power from resistance against powers that reduce it to an effect of the existing order. The work's affirmative element lies in its opening to beyond what exists, whose positivity it first generates. The experience of art is the experience both of its conditions of possibility and of the affront to those that it represents. The concept of art condenses the paradox of an achievement that has to turn against its own possibilities in favor of the impossible as the impossibility that is possible for achievement.

Art is that which brings forth a concept of art in asserting works that, while resisting their assimilation into the existing order, articulate themselves as affirmations of contingency, as figures of an opening to that indeterminacy and incommensurability marking off the truth of the space of facts. I call the universe of facts the dimension of reality that is overdetermined socially, politically, economically, historically, culturally, biologically, technically, and so on. Here the artwork struggles for its autonomy—in the field of factical codification, real heteronomy into which it remains in jeopardy of relapsing: "Artworks are able to appropriate their heterogeneous element, their entwinement with society, because they are themselves always at the same time something social. Nevertheless, art's autonomy, wrested painfully from society as well as socially derived in itself, has the potential of reversing into heteronomy; everything new is weaker than the accumulated ever-same, and it is ready to regress back into it."[05]

No matter how much art "refuses definition,"[06] it also demands one. Art is scarcely anything other than work on its own concept, the determination of what art is and ought to be. In the opening to where it has long since already been admitted, the dimension of constituted certainties and valencies, art is pushed to the limit not only of the space of facts but also of its concept and its form of appearance hitherto. Art contains a dynamic for bringing forth itself through works in a continual redefinition of what is to be understood by its concept. Art extends the concept of art by unbounding itself to its other that bounds it. Every artwork is a form of unbounding, an excess directed toward its implicit inconsistency.[07] It is an excess marking its unbounding from its border, its openness to formlessness, whose bearer it remains. Art is an assertion of form

35

generating itself in an opening to formlessness.[08] No matter whether this formlessness be society as an overly complex, intracontradictory space of facts (the zone of sociohistorico-symbolic evidence), or whether it be the point of inconsistency within this domain, the incommensurability commensurable with formlessness.

2. The artwork implies a surpassing and transgressing of its factual conditions.

"All artworks, even the affirmative, are a priori polemical." [09]
    Affirmation by the artwork is the affirmation of its polemical violence directed against everything that limits its claim to autonomy: constituted reality in its complexity and multiplicity, which Adorno calls society. Art exists only in the here and now of this one world without an exit, the world of facts. Art is not an escape from it; it formulates its claim to autonomy in the midst of the world of determinants in order, in an opening to heteronomy, to escape this world's phantasmagoric mistaking of itself. Just as there is freedom only under conditions of factual unfreedom, sovereign independence only under conditions of its absence, autonomy becomes a demand and necessity only in the field of factual heteronomy. Adorno never ceases to plead for the possibility of aesthetic autonomy in its opening to its impossibility. Thus he becomes the advocate of a possible impossibility. Art implies a "refusal of empirical facts." Art distances itself "from the empirical world," not by fleeing into a second, higher world, but by intensifying its relation to this empirical world. Art's "inescapable affirmative essence"[10] must turn against its distorted image, against the idealist temptation to locate art somewhere beyond the world of facts. Affirmation is not naïveté or approval.

of oneself, throwing oneself away" that leads to surrender of the ego as well as to the loss of form: "surfeit as form" becomes "deficit in form." The authentic assertion of form, however, opens itself as the form of formlessness in order at the same time to oppose it. Deleuze and Guattari have defined the task of art (as well as that of philosophy and science) in no other way: to open oneself to chaos without losing oneself in it. Cf. Theodor W. Adorno, Beethoven: Philosophie der Musik (Frankfurt am Main: Suhrkamp, 2004), 115, 224, as well as Gilles Deleuze and Félix Guattari, What Is Philosophy?, trans. Hugh Tomlinson and Graham Burchell (New York: Columbia University Press, 1994).

[08] Cf. Marcus Steinweg, Behauptungsphilosophie (Berlin: Merve, 2006).
[09] Adorno, "Toward a Theory of the Artwork," 177.

[10] Adorno, "Art, Society, Aesthetics," 2.
[11] Max Horkheimer and Theodor W. Adorno, Dialectic of Enlightenment: Philosophical Fragments, ed. Gunzelin Schmid Noerr, trans. Edmund Jephcott (Stanford, Calif.: Stanford University Press, 2002), xii.
[12] Theodor W. Adorno, Negative Dialectics, trans. W. B. Ashton (New York: Seabury Press, 1973), 15.
[13] Theodor W. Adorno, Critical Models: Interventions and Catchwords, trans. Henry W. Pickford (New York: Columbia University Press, 1998), 165.
[14] Adorno, "Toward a Theory of the Artwork," 182.

Affirmation is invention and construction. The artwork's
affirmative intensity implies a double gesture comprising the
acknowledgment of its historicity as well as the courage not to
enclose itself smugly within the critical, reflexive reassur-
ance of its resultant status, which demands its opening up to
the inconsistency of the web of determinants. Facts are nothing
but facts: art knows that knowledge is not everything, that the
artist's responsibility begins with building up an affirmative
resistance against all kinds of vulgar materialism and positivism, at the same time suspending all kinds of idealism, promis-
ing it a reality beyond this single, unique reality, in order
finally to dehistoricize it completely. Realism and idealism are
pseudoalternatives for the history of philosophy, for philosophical aesthetics, for art.

A "concept of history" as a "critique of philosophy" that
"does not seek to abandon philosophy itself," as we read in the
preface to the 1969 edition of <u>Dialectic of Enlightenment</u>,[11] has
its counterpart in the effort, "by way of the concept, to tran-
scend the concept"[12] as well as in an understanding of art that
conceives of itself, in view of its impossibility (heteronomy,
historicity), as possible (autonomous, universal). What holds
for the concept of a "true human being"—"He would be neither a
mere function of a whole, which is inflicted upon him so thor-
oughly that he cannot distinguish himself from it anymore, nor
would he simply retrench himself in his pure selfhood"—holds
also for the true artwork.[13] In the field of tension between
immanence and transcendence, the concept of art, along with that
of the subject, situates itself porously between the factual
social interconnections and their inconsistency, contact with
which opens up the chance of autonomy and freedom. That is the
affirmation achieved by the artwork, the acknowledgment of itself as an element of the empirical world as well as a figure of
its resistant opposition.

3. An artwork is something other than (merely) a document of
   its times.

"The distinction...between the artwork and the document holds
good insofar as it rejects works that are not in themselves determined by the law of form."[14]

Art was never anything other than consent to the fragility
of its times. Art does not come from a stable situation; it is
the experience of the inconsistency of its reality. Art exists
only as the experience of the porosity of the system of facts.
Therefore, for it, there cannot be any alliance with facts,
which does not mean that it disputes or misrecognizes their
power. But art does not exhaust itself in demonstrating this
non-misrecognition through the analytical power that is also im-
manent within it. As long as art does not surpass its knowledge,
it is not art. It would be nothing other than a self-reassurance

for the subject within the web of its critically commentated situation. Only an assertion of form that evades a narcissistic self-reassuring by articulating the transience of the certainty of facts succeeds in confronting the universal inconsistency that is the subject's proper time and proper place.[15]

More than being a document of its times, the artwork is a corruption of the zeitgeist and the sociohistoric texture from which it indeed arises. If a work were nothing other than the result of its conditions and reducible to its determinants, it would not be a work. The essential feature of an artwork is that it inscribes a resistance in the reality to which it belongs by appearing in it as something incommensurable. What distances it from the document is this excess that alienates it from its status as a fact, since this status indicates the ontological fragility of the texture of facts. The artwork's assertion of form disputes neither its origins in the world of facts nor its existence in this world; it resists simply its reduction to it by appearing in it as something unforeseen. The appearance of the work shows it to be the arena for a conflict between the existing order and that which threatens to topple it. Whereas the document is for transporting information, for communicating and archiving it, the artwork is a questioning of information, communication, and archiving. The insistence that "the arts will not fit into any gapless concept of art" says in the first place that there is no such gapless concept.[16] Since art practices the permanent re-destabilization of all stable forms and concepts, it compels for each artwork its appropriate concept whose universality experiences its corrective through the singularity of the individual work in order, at the same time, to point beyond it to its universality. The artwork's universality must take up the singularity of the individual result like an uninvited guest. If it does not do this, it is a fiction of universality. True universality is one that affirms the singular status of artworks instead of negating it. The artwork is universal by building up a form, beyond its status as a document, that is held hovering above the abyss of formlessness, which in turn points to the incommensurability of the world of facts. No work is grounded in any sort of ontological principle. Rather, it is an assertion that, although such a principle does not exist, the

---

[15] To be a subject means to surpass and transgress the horizon of facts in order—in the assertion of a new form, the form of the subject—to give space to the experience of a primordial inner turmoil, which is the truth of the subject. I call this inner turmoil the incommensurability of a life that, as the life of a subject, reaches beyond its representation as subject in the field of aesthetic, social, political, and cultural evidence. The subject articulates this distance not in retrospect. It _is_ nothing other than the distance that it articulates vis-à-vis the authority of facts.

[16] Adorno, "Art, Society, Aesthetics," 2.

[17] Adorno, "Toward a Theory of the Artwork," 183.

[18] Ibid., 196.

[19] Theodor W. Adorno, Einleitung in die Musiksoziologie: Zwölf theoretische Vorlesungen (Frankfurt am Main: Suhrkamp, 1975), 238.

form fought for by the work opposes mere arbitrariness through
evidence evident only to the form.

4. Art articulates a difference from the texture of facts.

"Foreignness to the world is an element of art: Whoever perceives it other than as foreign fails to perceive it at all."[17]
    Art is an assertion of difference. In the zone of familiar-
ity, art appears as something unfamiliar. The artwork has an
alienness that makes it into something unfamiliar in the domain
of established certainties. With sovereign independence it
resists its appropriation by communicative intelligence. The
"adequate assimilation" of its reception, as Adorno says, is the
"communication of the uncommunicable."[18] Instead of primarily
communicating, art is an invention and a construction. Its pro-
gressivism is due to the will to assert a form that makes precise the universal formlessness (the exterior, the real, chaos,
the incommensurable, or, following Adorno, the nonidentical or
elementary). Art exists only as an assertion of form that accel-
erates beyond what is known while refusing to assimilate itself
into any sort of nature. The alliance with anything natural is
necessarily regressive. Such an alliance enters a coalition with
a metaphysics of the origin that is at work in every attempt to
stabilize the present by turning back to the past. Art is the
surpassing and transgressing of naturalism and originism. What
is new in art is too new to be as old as an origin. The artwork
neither articulates its intimacy with nature and origins, nor
does it enter into solidarity with the zeitgeist. Art exists
only as a conflict with its times. Every persuasive artwork
comes from the future; it never arises from the past. Weak art
can be recognized through its sentimentality, nostalgia, adoration of the past—in short, through its inability to make the
future precise. Instead of competing with documentation and historical work, it is a matter of giving a form to the formlessness of tomorrow today, here and now. Art implies the courage to
give answers to questions that do not preexist. There is no art
beyond the affirmation of something new. No matter, as demanded
by the Aristotelian perspective, how much it remains tied to
what exists, no matter how much it remains embedded in the material texture, nevertheless the new rewrites it by appearing in
this texture as something unforeseen.
    The artwork implies an "antithetical critical element"[19]
that allows it to reflect its conditions. It must not exhaust
itself in such reflection, however, since it includes, like
any positing, assertion of form and decision, an element of
proflective blindness, an element evading its self-understanding
and its self-reassuring. A minimum of blindness, a minimum of
tendentiousness and interest, a minimum of uncontrollability
and violence is still part of the most careful analysis. If it
denies that, it is naive and offers itself as such as an object

of analysis that convicts it of an implicit blindness. Now art does not have much to do with mistrust, conviction, and police zeal. Its critical power correlates with an affirmation resembling an ontological consent. Obviously, both elements cross over in the artwork: consent and not being in agreement, affirmation and negativity. The political aspect of art lies in turning equally to both elements, on the one hand, refusing to neutralize its critical power in a merely blind affirmation, in order, on the other hand, to keep the certainty alive within it that there can be no art that could, or even should, get rid of its blindness, since it marks the work's opening to something unknown and new. That is what distinguishes it from journalism—this opening to its blindness as a productive power. Blindness, ambivalence, and truth mark the status of incommensurability of a world that has begun to believe in itself as if in a fact. There is only one world; there is no second world, no world behind this one, no utopian place. But this one world without an exit is in no way identical with the intelligence it supplies about itself in the form of images, language, information. Rather, it has an incommensurability that withdraws from any direct appearance. It denotes nothing other than the inconsistency of the universe of consistency that we call reality. The affirmative trait of the artwork sews it to this incommensurability, which inscribes itself as a resistance in every religiosity of the facts.

The alertness and care of art, its political nature, become visible in its resistance against the temptation to turn itself into journalism, in its resistance against the power of facts, on the one hand, and against the aesthetic, always idealist mistaking of itself in the phantasma of pure art, on the other. Art exists only in the sphere of economic, cultural, social, and political overdetermination. Here it must articulate its distance from everything that limits its claim to autonomy.

5. The artwork is the affirmation of this difference.

As an affirmation of difference, art affirms the hyperbolism characterizing it, which obliges it to respect the incommensurable rather than facts that misrecognize their fictitious status. In the eighty-second aphorism in Minima Moralia, Adorno describes the opening of thinking to the inconsistency of facts:
    While thought relates to facts and moves by criticizing them,
    its movement depends no less on the maintenance of distance.
    It expresses exactly what is, precisely because what is is
    never quite as thought expresses it. Essential to it is an
    element of exaggeration, of over-shooting the object, of
    self-detachment from the weight of the factual, so that in-
    stead of merely reproducing being it can, at once rigorous
    and free, determine it. Thus every thought resembles play,
    with which Hegel no less than Nietzsche compared the work

of the mind. The unbarbaric side of philosophy is its tacit awareness of the element of irresponsibility, of blitheness springing from the volatility of thought, which forever escapes what it judges. Such licence is resented by the positivistic spirit and put down to mental disorder. Divergence from the facts becomes mere wrongness, the moment of play a luxury in a world where the intellectual functions have to account for their every moment with a stop-watch. But as soon as thought repudiates its inviolable distance and tries with a thousand subtle arguments to prove its literal correctness, it founders. If it leaves behind the medium of virtuality, of anticipation that cannot be wholly fulfilled by any single piece of actuality; in short, if instead of interpretation it seeks to become mere statement, everything it states becomes, in fact, untrue. Its apologetics, inspired by uncertainty and a bad conscience, can be refuted at every step by demonstrating the non-identity which it will not acknowledge, yet which alone makes it thought. If, on the other hand, it tried to claim its distance as a privilege, it would act no better, but would proclaim two kinds of truth, that of the facts and that of ideas. That would be to decompose truth itself, and truly to denigrate thought. Distance is not a safety-zone but a field of tension.[20]

What Adorno says about thinking holds in the same degree for art. Art is a form of exaggeration in that it affirms the "difference from facts" as the condition of its possibility. [21] Art exists only as a hyperbolic (because unreserved) affirmation of its hyperbolism. Positivism, which is devoted to the facts like proven certainties, understands nothing as long as it reduces thinking (as well as art) to a sequence of certain steps, robbing it of its fantasy. It could almost be said that there is no thinking that is not art, if art implies the excess, the surpassing and transgressing of the authority of facts. The artistic character of thinking would mark its relatedness to a practice of articulation of the self in the world that pronounces the imperative of literalness in order to provoke a disturbance in the midst of established, correct facts by inventing new (aesthetic) forms and new concepts. The distance from what is correct and well known, from the factual and the firmly existing, is the element in which art and philosophy come to themselves, without relying on arriving punctually. Ontological unpunctuality is inherent within the human subject. The subject is never simultaneous, never on time, never identical with itself. Derrida has thought of this incongruence of the subject as an irreducible deferment (différance). Adorno's concept of

[20] Theodor W. Adorno, Minima Moralia: Reflections from Damaged Life, trans. E. F. N. Jephcott (London: NLB, 2003), 126–27.

[21] Cf. Alexander García Düttmann, Philosophy of Exaggeration, trans. James Philips (London and New York: Continuum, 2007).

the nonidentical marks this rift. Rift or gulf, incision in the subject, these are hallmarks of art and philosophy insofar as they resist positivist and idealist ideology. Art's affirmation is the affirmation of this incision, which, by alienating it from the zone of facts, keeps every subject cut, nonidentical with itself, that is, free and unfree at the same time. Autonomous and heteronomous like the artwork, which remains a result of society and history while at the same time flying over them, entirely in the sense of flying over (survol) of which Deleuze and Guattari speak in order to articulate the difference between becoming and history. The movement of becoming is transhistorical in that it flies over the merely historical but without losing contact with it. The territory flown over is constitutive for the subject flying over qua subject flown over. Society—as denoted by Adorno—has penetrated every artwork, whether the artist wanted it to or not. But nevertheless it affirms a certain distance from it, an infinitesimal freedom that can scarcely be proved, like the aesthetic, nonobjective evidence inherent in the plausibility of a persuasive artwork.

6. This affirmation takes place as an assertion of form.

How is the place of the work within the social field to be determined? How do the production of art, art criticism, art studies, and philosophy relate to one another? Is there a political commission for an artwork? Is art necessarily critical—critical of institutions, the market, ideology? Or does an artwork put certain limits upon criticism and its good conscience, which make of it a risky, necessarily affirmative practice? Does its sense lie in these categories of resistance and subversion invariably associated with the artwork, but also in a self-calming that enables the artist to participate in the political game without genuine commitment, so that political consciousness takes on the function of a depoliticization that has not been admitted? How affirmative must an artwork be in order to be subversive or political?

In order to be an assertion of form and truth, art and philosophy must refuse the "order of real politics."[22] That is the order of the possible, of pragmatism and its practical cleverness, of situational intelligence. It is the order of phrónesis, as Aristotle says, the dimension of diplomatic reason.[23] Aristotle calls phrónesis intelligence in particularity, in unfreedom, intelligence that operates in relation to the situation in which it decides and acts. As Gadamer ceaselessly underscored, it is the principle of hermeneutics, reason that ponders and weighs up. That brings it close to the pragmatic estimation of doxá, of sound common sense. Art and philosophy have an inherent absolute resistance to doxá and phrónesis because they compel the subject to decelerate, to brake itself, to renounce power. Philosophy and art want to erect the subject

as a power of assertion that resists defusing by <u>doxá</u> and
<u>phrónesis</u>. The subject truly decides and acts only by neglecting
its situation, ignoring and transcending it by puncturing the
texture of facts. Subject is nothing other than the name for
this puncturing and hyperbole, which it necessarily represents.
Hence the mistrust of a subject of such self-authorization because it resists its own defusing by the spirit of facts.

Philosophy and art move as radical forms of assertion assured by no universal principle and beyond the order of fea-
sibility, not in order to be more estranged from the world or
reality than politics within the order of real politics, but
in order to place the intensity of their assertion in another
horizon, in a horizon of infinitude and impossibility where the
subject resists absorption by mere interests or <u>inclinations</u>, as
Kant put it.[24] Art and philosophy are forms of self-acceleration
of a desire to assert that breaks through the consensual horizons of discussion, argumentation, communication, explanation,
justification, and reflective self-securing. Art and philosophy
exist only as this breakthrough, as a force of surpassing and
transgressing the horizon, which punctures the horizon of the
possible through to the dimension of the impossible that is the
dimension of truth.

Truth is not founded by philosophy and art. Truth can only
be asserted. Truth cannot be grounded. Truth eventuates when
the subject alienates itself from the symbolic order, from its
sociocultural integrity as well as phantasms of the imaginary.
There is truth at the moment when philosophy and art touch the
impossible—pure virtuality, the real, or chaos—by risking a
transgression of the horizon.[25] Philosophy and art are forms
of realization of truths that do not preexist. It cannot be a
matter of finding truths; it is a matter of inventing them,
of producing truth. "'Truth' is never there of itself or in
itself,'" and as such decipherable, "but contested and fought
for," says Heidegger.[26] Such a truth, insofar as it is the
product of a contesting, struggling subject of assertion, is
therefore not relative in the simple sense of the word. Philosophy and art assert truth (art asserts truth by asserting a form)

[22] Alain Badiou, <u>Metapolitics</u>, trans.
Jason Barker (London: Verso, 2003),
110.

[23] On the interplay between <u>phróne-
sis</u> (practical intelligence)
and <u>sophrosyné</u> (moderation), see
Aristotle, <u>Ethica Nicomachea</u>, liber
VI, 1140 b 10ff.

[24] There is this misunderstanding
concerning the concept of form: it
is often thought that form creates
clarity. That is an error. Form is
clarity that produces disorder!
Chaos. Hence the widespread wari-
ness of form, in art as well as
in thinking. Hence the ubiquitous
decision in favor of diffuseness.
Because diffuseness cooperates with
transparency, whereas the assertion
of form risks a clarity that does
not betray the extent of factual
intransparency.

[25] On the "identification of truth
with the real," see Alenka Zupancic,
<u>The Shortest Shadow: Nietzsche's
Philosophy of the Two</u> (Cambridge,
Mass.: MIT Press, 2003), 92.

[26] Martin Heidegger, <u>Parmenides</u>,
Gesamtausgabe, vol. 54 (Frankfurt
am Main: V. Klostermann, 1992), 25.

by withdrawing from the relativism of the truth of facts and the regime of proof and argumentative assurance.[27] Philosophy and art do not assert any facts. They constitute truths that corrupt the order of facts. The locus of truth cannot be found within the universe of facts. That is the utopianism of truth, that it is as such deranged, somewhere else, that it bursts the register of facts, that it insists on another place not on the map of this topology.

7. Every assertion of form is indebted to making contact with formlessness.

"The concept of tension frees itself from the suspicion of being formalistic in that, by pointing up dissonant experiences or antinomical relations in the work, it names the element of 'form' in which form gains its substance by virtue of its relation to its other."[28]

The tension that is part of an artwork allows it to mediate that which cannot be mediated. That is the dialectical, aporetic trait of the work that makes it into an arena for the bracketing of form with formlessness. In a letter to Thomas Mann dated August 1, 1950, Adorno, anticipating his concept of negative dialectic, says of the "writer's dilemma" something that pertains to the dilemma of art in general: "one either defers to the tact of language, which almost inevitably involves a loss of precision in the matter, or one privileges the latter over the former and thereby does violence to the language it-self. Every sentence is effectively an aporia, and every successful utterance a happy deliverance, a realization of the impossible, a reconciliation of subjective intention with objective spirit, whereas the essence consists precisely in the diremption of both."[29] Almost every sentence in Aesthetic Theory articulates with the means of language the aporetic essence of art. The challenge lies in putting into words "the constitutive relation of art to what itself is not, to what is not the pure spontaneity of the subject."[30] Once again, the ambiguity of the artwork caught between a desire for reconcilia-tion and its inexorable irreconcilability, art as an oscillation between identity and difference, between form and formlessness, becomes apparent. It is this between that defines the status of the artistic assertion of form as a form of formlessness as well as a formlessness of form. In order to avoid aestheticism, art must acknowledge its self-extension to the nonartistic sphere of facts. In order, in turn, not to instrumentalize it-self in the image of sociopolitical commitment or in moralism, it insists on aesthetic autonomy. Instead of choosing between violence and nonviolence, art votes for itself as the operator of this interstitial between that can scarcely be reconciled in a speculative synthesis. Every assertion of form mediates itself with its (social) other because the other has long

since leaped ahead of it. And yet art must not exhaust itself
in an adoration of the other or the incommensurable in order
finally to sacrifice its capacity to form to a religiosity of
formlessness. Art is that which endures the conflict of form and
formlessness, thus articulating it.

8. Making contact with formlessness corresponds to making
   contact with truth.

If art has something to do with truth, then it does so in the
following sense: instead of revealing truths like facts, the
artwork is the locus of the separating of truth from facts insofar as facts, in the light of their uncovering, obscure the cha-
otic abyss or nonground that itself does not appear in the light
of facts and, by definition, cannot appear. To touch a truth
means to make contact with this nonground, which Castoriadis
(as does Žižek),[31] following Hegel, associates with the <u>night
of the world</u>. In a well-known passage from the Jena System Draft
from 1805–6, Hegel casts this ghostly scenario concerning the
subject qua subject:

> The human being is this night, this empty nothingness which
> contains everything in its simplicity, a wealth of infinitely
> many ideas, images, of which none simply occurs to it or
> which are not present. This [is] the night, the interior of
> nature that exists here—<u>pure self</u>. In phantasmagoric ideas,
> all around it is night; here a bloody head then suddenly
> shoots forth, there another white shape, both disappearing
> just as suddenly. We see this night when we look a human
> being in the eye, into a night which becomes <u>terrible</u>; the
> night of the world dangles here before us.[32]

The "night of the world" is another name for the chaos that
the subject's subjectivity is. The subject's confrontation with
itself demands of it that it open itself up to this zone, which
is both overly rich and void. It is the domain of something real
that has not yet assumed the form of a reality, the dimension
of an "abyss" marking the "infinite possibility of representation."[33] The artwork, as well as the subject, is related to

[27] "Relativism, no matter how progressive its bearing, has at all times
been linked with moments of reaction, beginning with the sophists'
availability to the more powerful
interests" (Adorno, <u>Negative
Dialectics</u>, 37).

[28] Theodor W. Adorno, "Paralipomena,"
in <u>Aesthetic Theory</u>, 292.

[29] Theodor W. Adorno and Thomas
Mann, <u>Correspondence, 1943–1955</u>,
ed. Christoph Gödde and Thomas
Sprecher, trans. Nicholas Walker
(Cambridge, England: Polity,
2006), 62.

[30] Theodor W. Adorno, "Theories of
the Origin of Art," in <u>Aesthetic
Theory</u>, 326.

[31] Cf. Slavoj Žižek, <u>Die Nacht der
Welt: Psychoanalyse und Deutscher
Idealismus</u> (Frankfurt am Main:
Fischer, 1998).

[32] G. W. F. Hegel, <u>Jenaer Realphiloso-
phie</u>, ed. J. Hoffmeister (Hamburg:
Felix Meiner, 1969), 180–81.

[33] Cornelius Castoriadis, <u>Fenêtre sur
le chaos</u> (Paris: Editions du Seuil,
2007), 152.

this abyss, to this lack of focus that makes its stabilization within the established field of reality more difficult. Truth is a title for this instability, which tears the work as well as the subject beyond itself toward the night of the indefinite. Therefore, instead of comprehensibility, clarity is inherent in art because clarity evokes the limit of what can be comprehended. The artwork's transparency opens it up to an intransparency, which is originarily part of it.

To make chaos, the incommensurable, the exterior, the non-identical precise means articulating this transparency toward intransparency. In this sense, art is an assertion of form by tailoring a form to the opening to formlessness, a form that relates the subject of this measured tailoring to the immeasurable. One must gather the courage to combine the always headless assertion that the artwork remains with the clarity of an unassured making-precise that evades the dictates of comprehensibility and communication. The work's assertion is not headless simply because it is subjective or arbitrary. No matter how much every assertion comes from the artist-subject's indeterminate subjectivity, just as much does it refuse the expressive gesture of ego-expression (on this Badiou has said what is necessary) [34] and the metaphysics of interiority associated with it. The work's assertion of form denies itself the narcissism of making itself into an enigma, a procedure characteristic of bad art.

Inherent in the artwork is that it does not conceal anything and has nothing to hide because it has already long since been adjacent to opacity. As a "window on chaos" and "representation of the abyss" art is "nothing phenomenal" but "transparent": "There is never anything in it that is hidden behind something else."[35] Castoriadis is right to separate art—that which he calls "great art"—from the temptation to weaken the subject's self, from the power of diffuseness as well as from appeals of the zeitgeist that reduce it to a documentary reflex. The work's transparency includes a transcendence to something beyond critical reflection. The work neither bends to the esotericism of critical evidence (in order finally to assimilate itself into journalism), nor does it enter a coalition with the obscurantism of diffuseness or any kind of metaphysics of the artist.

9. Art's making contact with truth opens it to universality.

With art it is always a matter of tearing the work's consistency from a universal inconsistency, of producing a visibility lacking any self-evidence. Therefore, the work's appearance is a surprise because its evidence is of the order of the nonevident. Art exists at the moment when this appearance tears a hole in the web of facts in order to darken the evidence of instituted realities, not through obscurantism or blacking-out, but through clarity, through a surfeit of evidence. The moment of this evidence, which demands concepts that are not at hand, is the moment when the work's necessity shines forth while the subject is seeking its motives. The artwork has the power to disturb through clarity, to suspend the subject's certainties, "to suspend reality,"[36] as Deleuze once said. There has never been art that entered into a coalition with reality. Art is resistance against that which is, not in the name of what ought to be, but in the name of the portion of established reality that has remained nameless. In the artwork, recognized realities communicate with this resistance, denoting its ontological transience: the formlessness that resists its valid formalization. Instead of giving space to a dialectical reconciliation, the work is the place where poles that cannot be mediated cross. It marks the crossing of form and formlessness, while asserting a form that acknowledges chaos. The artwork's autonomy remains indebted to its heteronomy. It does not appear from nothingness as if it were without conditions, but because it articulates the infinitesimal distance from its conditions.[37] An artwork behaves toward its objective reality necessarily in a destructive way. It destroys the space of its reality because it lends to an inconsistency a consistency that demonstrates to acknowledged realities their arbitrariness.

These realities are arbitrary because their consistency is limited to the function of covering up an inconsistency that is universal contingency. The artwork, however, marks the threshold to inconsistency, which is the threshold between the order of facts and the dimension of truth. Instead of opening up to a second world which in some sense or other would be more real than "reality," it opens itself to reality in its valency of incommensurability. The work does not decide either in favor of the real or in favor of reality. It opens itself to the disturbing truth that reality is already the real, that every certainty, every fact, every solidity hovers above the abyss of an inconsistency. The work articulates itself as a construction held above this abyss. It distinguishes itself from the fictions of fact by having its function reside neither in covering up nor in making inconsistency livable. Inherent in the real is that it

[34] Alain Badiou, Dritter Entwurf eines Manifests für den Affirmationismus, ed. Frank R. Ruda and Jan Völker (Berlin: Merve, 2007).

[35] Castoriadis, Fenêtre sur le chaos, 153.

[36] Gilles Deleuze, "Erschöpft," in Quadrat, Geister-Trio: Stücke für das Fernsehen, by Samuel Beckett (Frankfurt am Main: Suhrkamp, 1996), 56.

[37] This distance turns creation into an act in the Lacanian sense, a deed that cannot be justified by anything, neither legitimate nor illegitimate. The act as a reality or creatio ex nihilo includes that it remains related to the "abyss in

reality," the hole in being, that is, to nothingness (Jacques Lacan, Das Seminar, Buch IV: Die Objektbeziehung, 1956-1957 [Vienna: Turia & Kant, 2003], 23). Cf. Lacan, Das Seminar, Buch VII: Die Ethik der Psychoanalyse, 1959-1960 (Weinheim: Quadriga, 1996), 143ff. The "hole of being" is Sartre's formula for nothingness. Cf. Jean-Paul Sartre, Being and Nothingness: An Essay on Phenomenological Ontology, trans. Hazel E. Barnes (New York: Citadel Press, 1969), 55. On the relationship between Sartre and Lacan, see Andreas Cremonini, Die Durchquerung des Cogito: Lacan contra Sartre (Munich: Fink, 2003).

remains invisible, or to employ Wittgensteinian categories, the real <u>shows</u> itself, and this showing is of the order of reporting the unspeakable. That is the difference between the factual thing and the artwork. The factual thing remains tied to the dimension of what is given, whereas the artwork gives witness to the questionability of the authorities of facts. Thus it opens itself to a void, which the consciousness of facts unceasingly tries to fill. Instead of bending to the existing order, the artwork makes contact with the inconsistency in the realities of facts. As a touching of the untouchable, it marks the threshold to something unknown, whose ontological status consists in not existing.[38]

Translated from the German by Michael Eldred, Cologne

[38] Badiou has described art as a "construction of the visibility of this nonexistence" (<u>Dritter Entwurf</u>, 35), in order finally, in the section of his <u>Logiques des mondes</u> dedicated to Derrida, to short-circuit <u>inexistance</u> (he writes it accordingly with <u>a</u>) with <u>différance</u>: "inexistance = différance. Pourquoi pas?" Why not, because <u>différance</u> marks the distance in being, the gap in presence, the rift in the subject. Cf. Alain Badiou, <u>Logiques des mondes: L'être et l'événement</u>, 2 (Paris: Éditions du Seuil, 2006), 570–71, as well as Badiou, <u>Peti panthéon portatif</u> (Paris: Fabrique, 2008), 117–33. Why not take this risk of an ontological narrowing that equates <u>différance</u> with <u>inexistence/inexistance</u>? For it is also equally clear that the hiatus in consciousness or the subject (i.e., in being itself) is called by the early Hegel the "night of the world," by Nietzsche "becoming," by Heidegger "hiddenness," by Sartre the "hole of freedom," by Lacan the "real," by Bataille the "heterogeneous," by Blanchot the "exterior," by Deleuze and Guattari "chaos." It is always a matter of thinking presence as absence or withdrawal or originary lethe, as "originary forgetting," as Agamben puts it, a forgetting that marks the contested compossibility of the incompossible, the primal conflict between identity and difference (cf. Giorgio Agamben, "Tradition de l'immémorial," in <u>La Puissance de la pensée</u>: Essais et conférences [Paris: Payot & Rivages, 2006], 129).

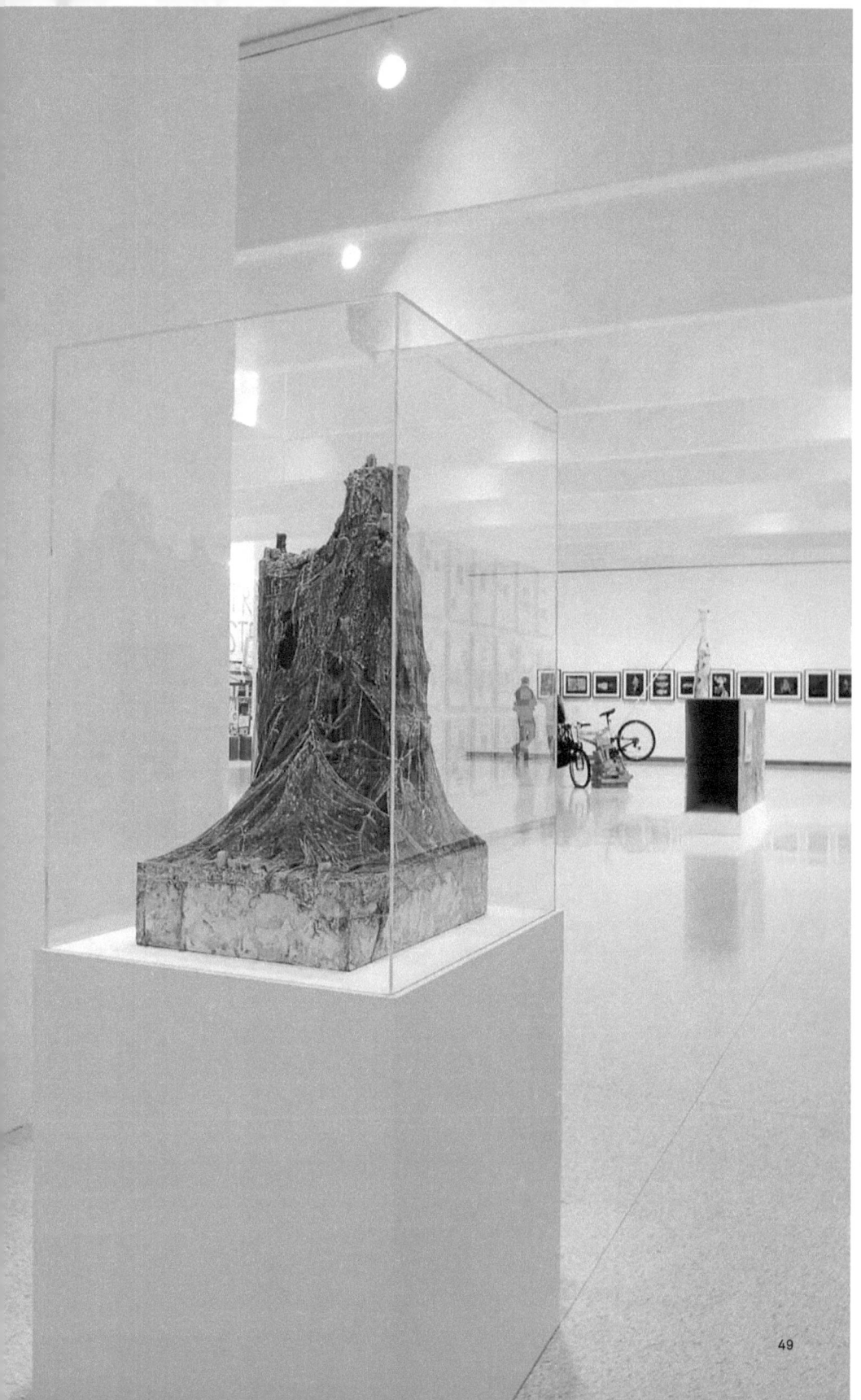

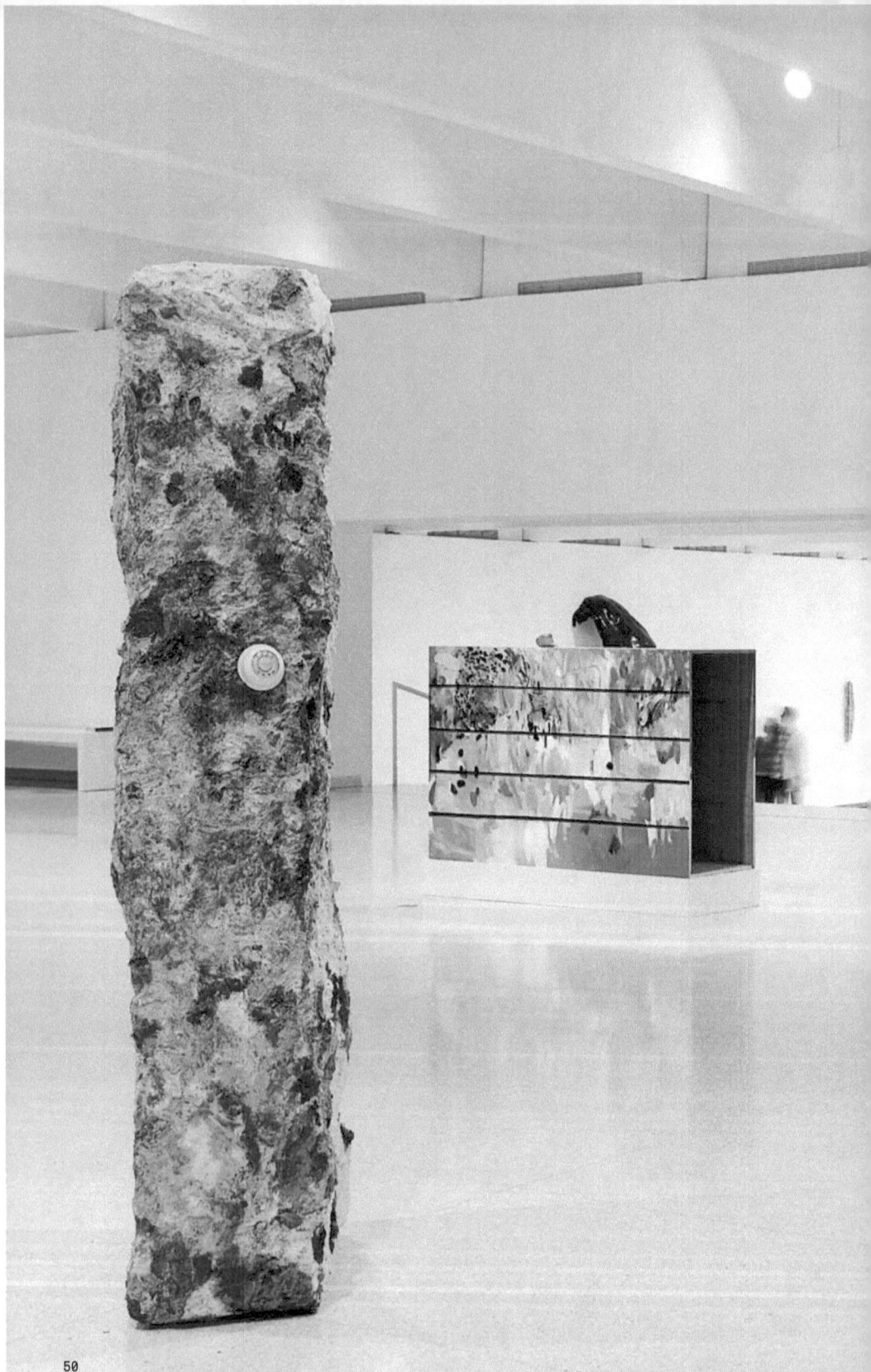

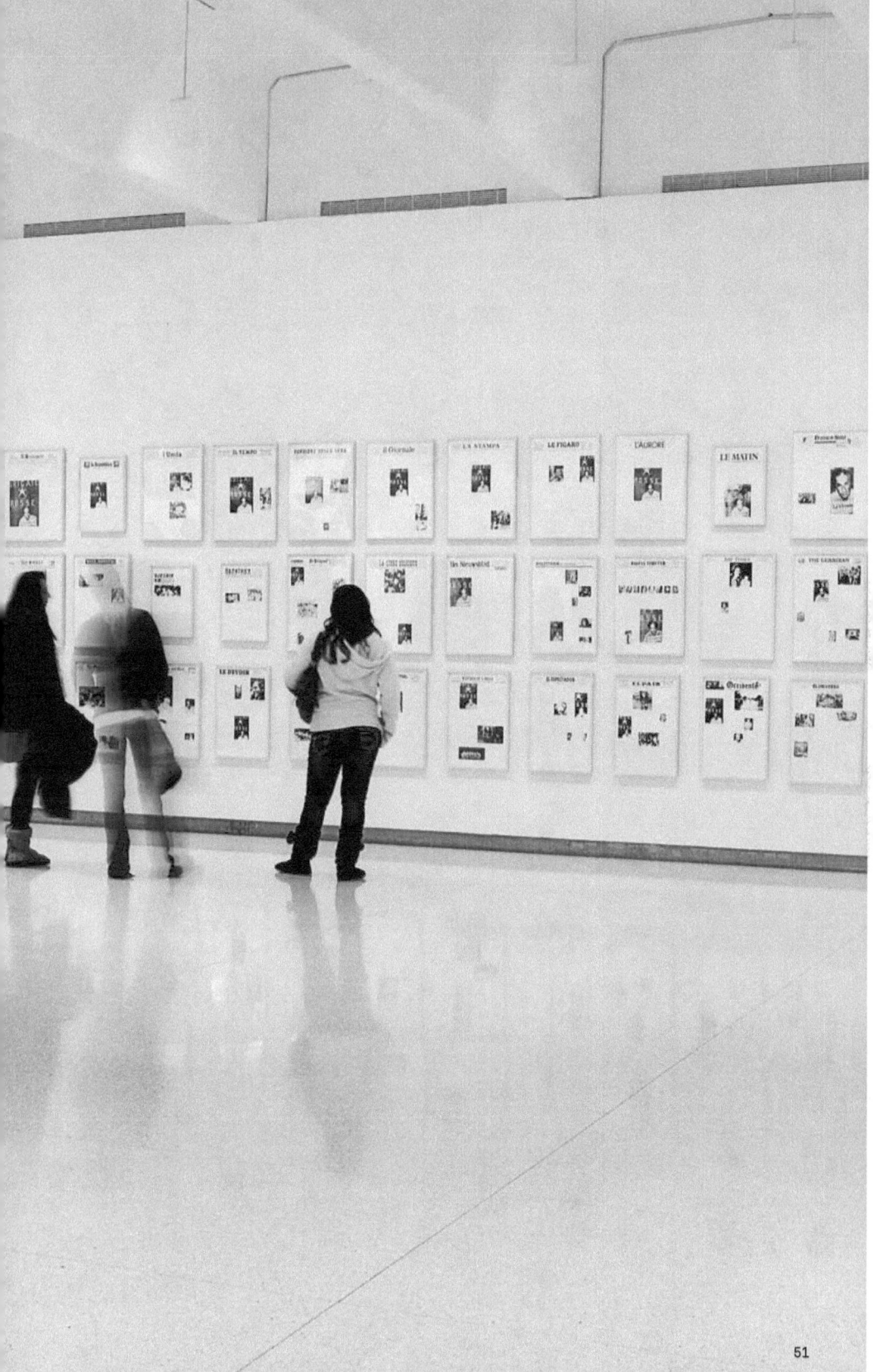

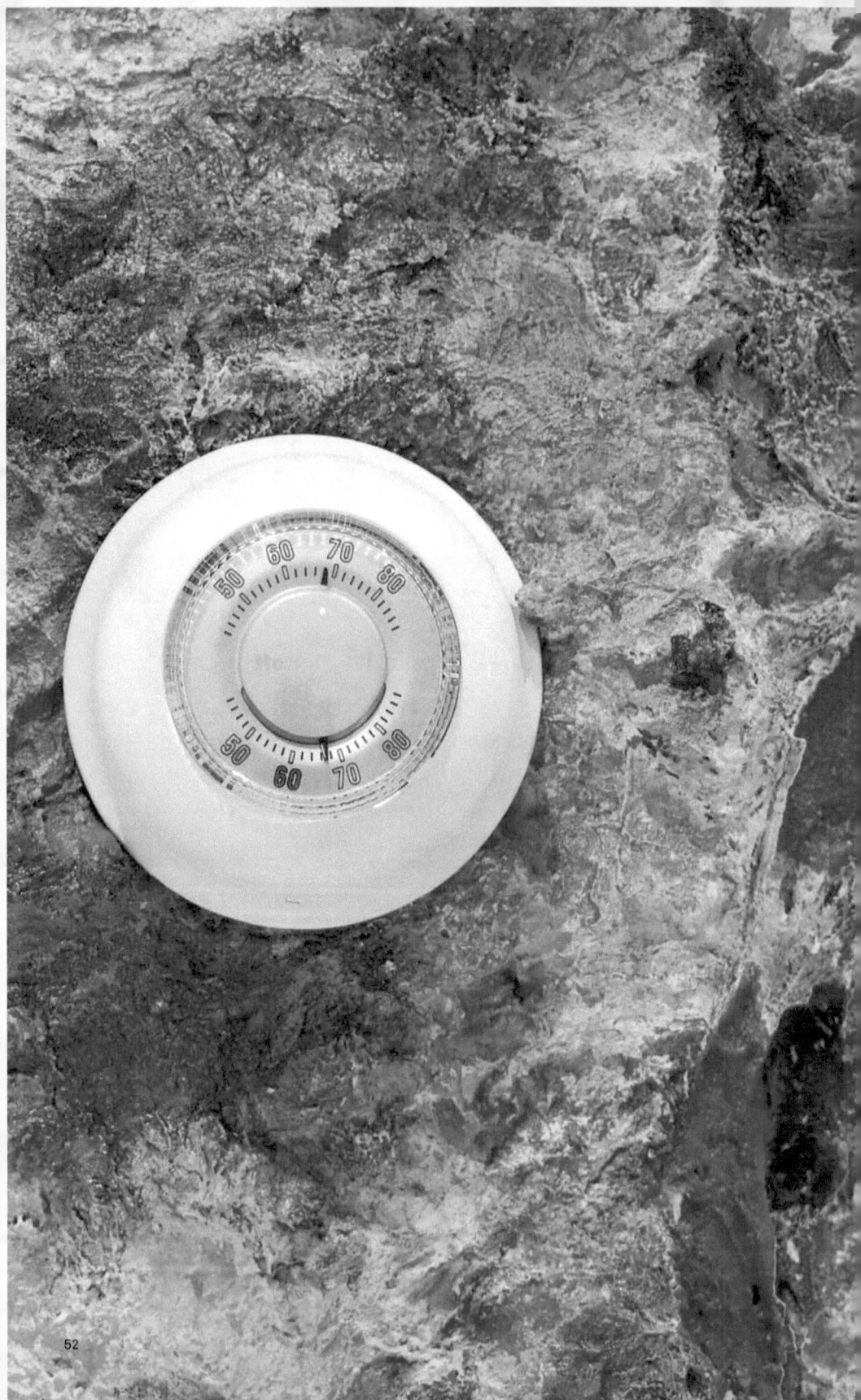

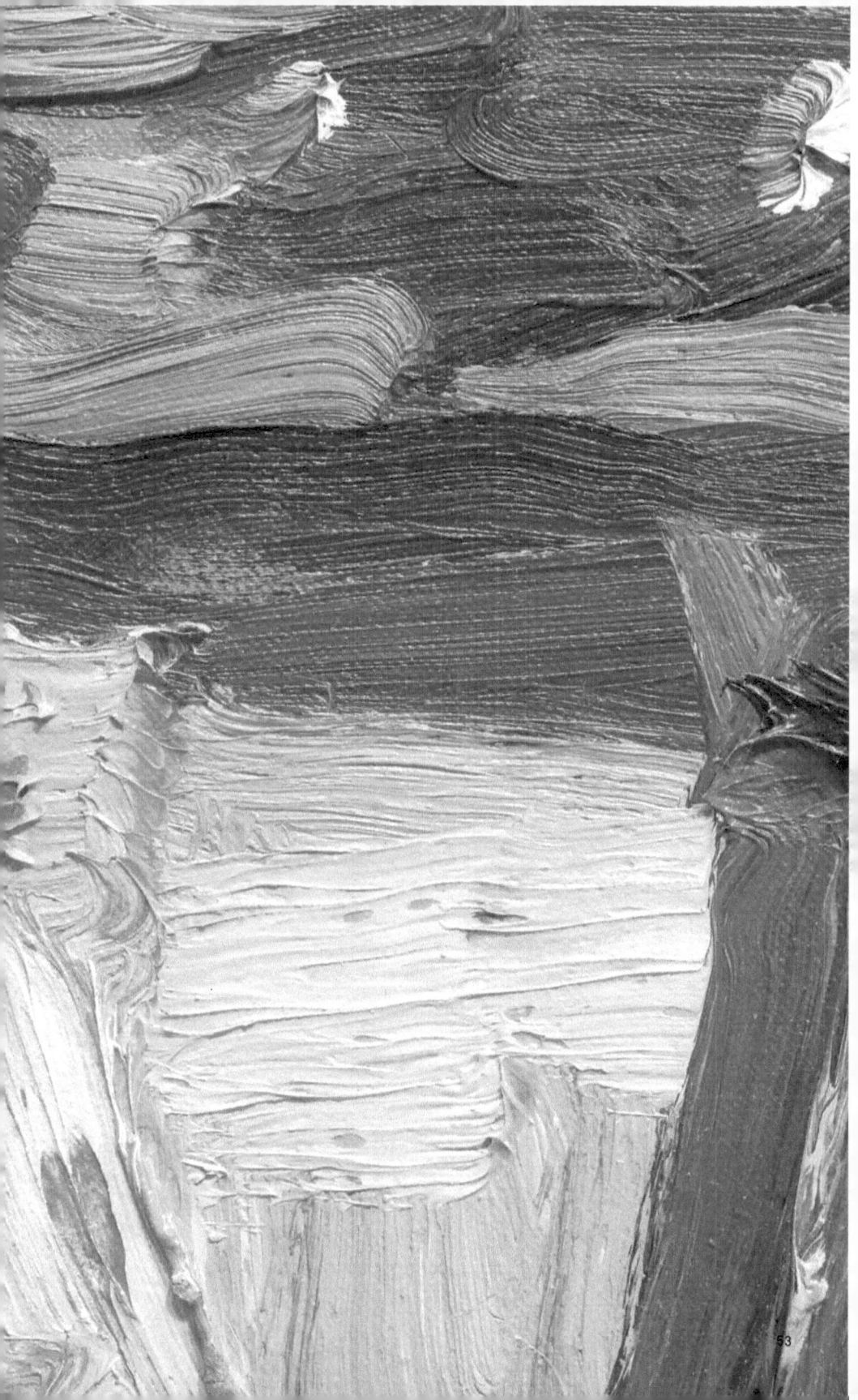

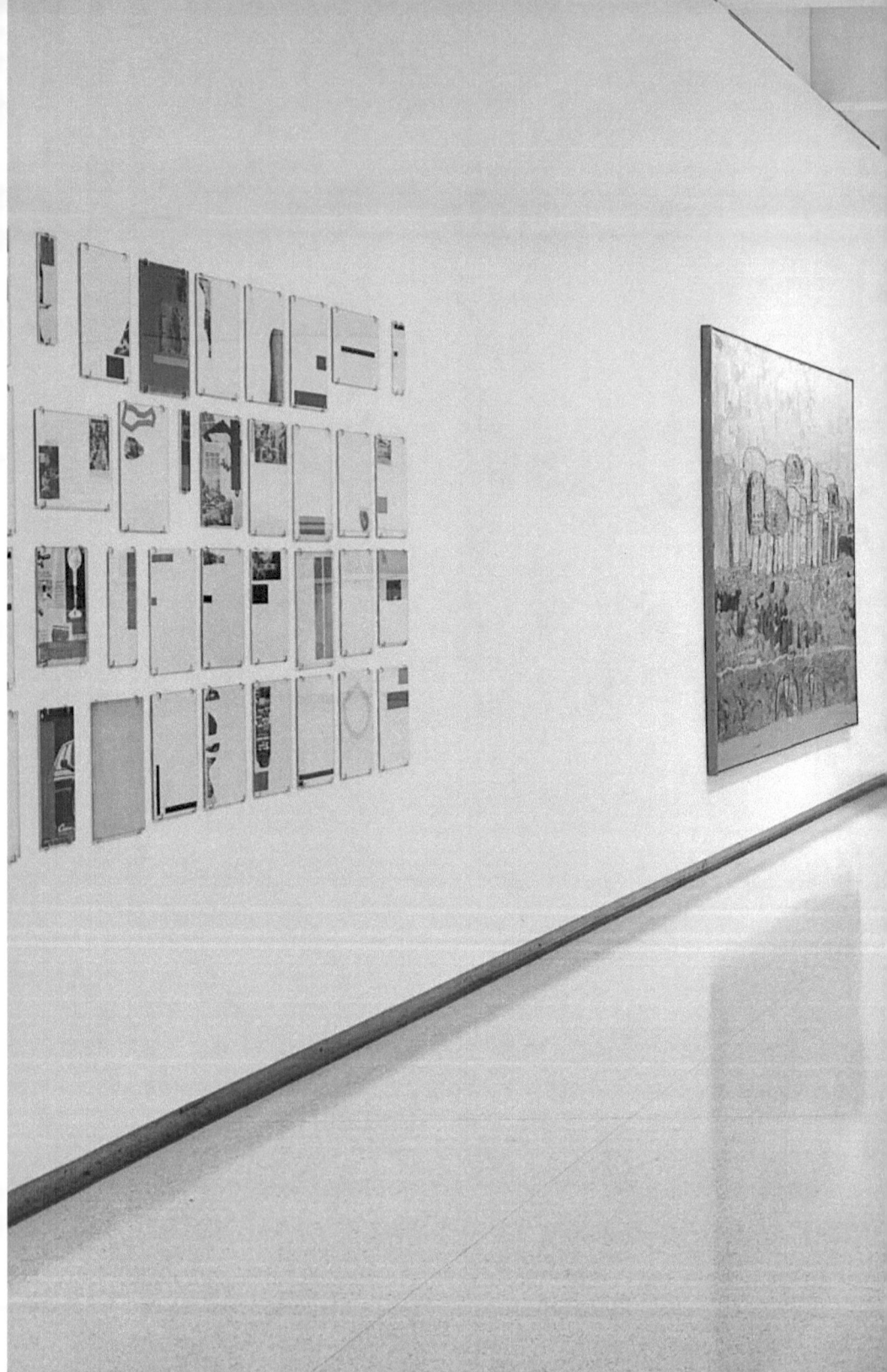

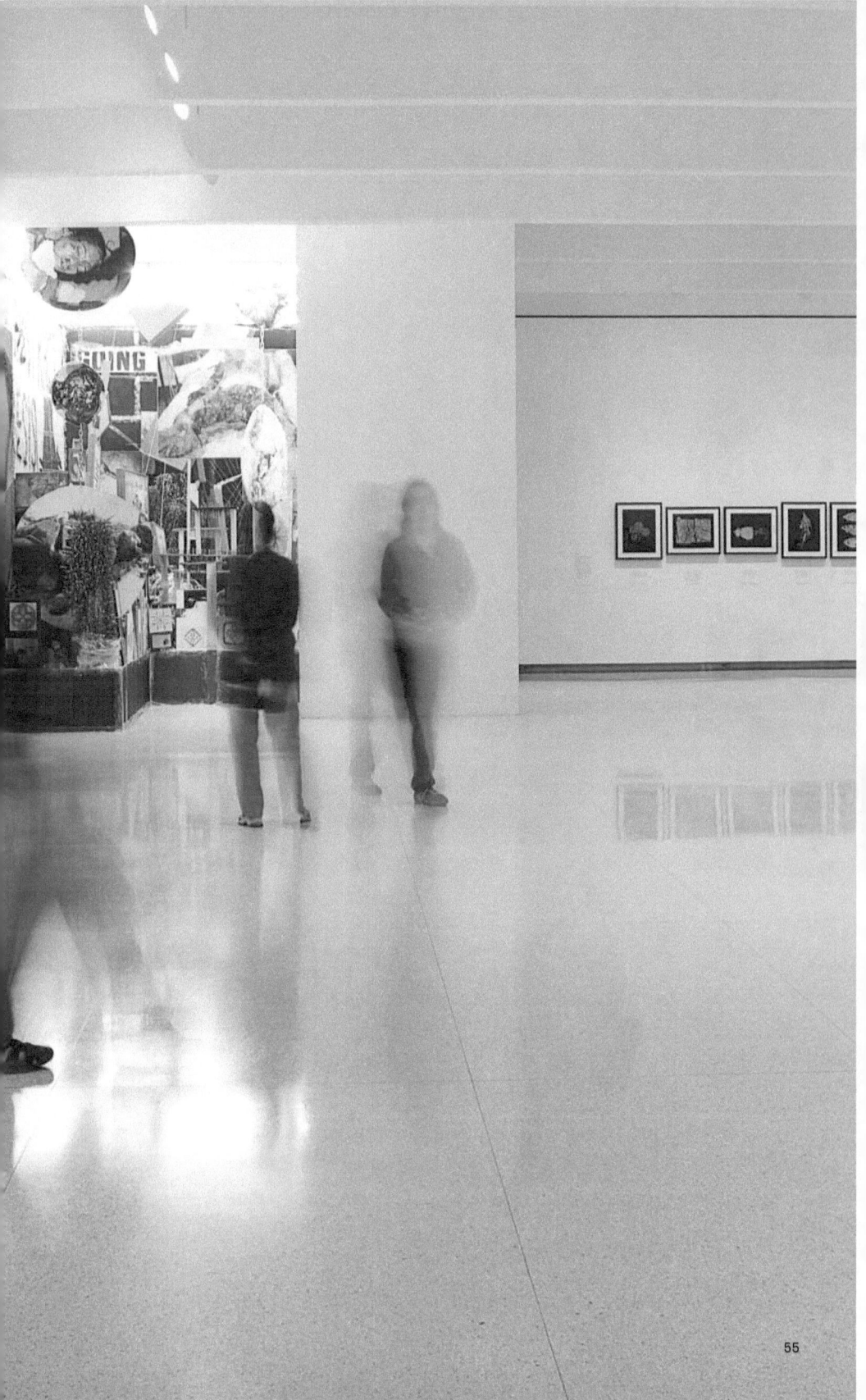

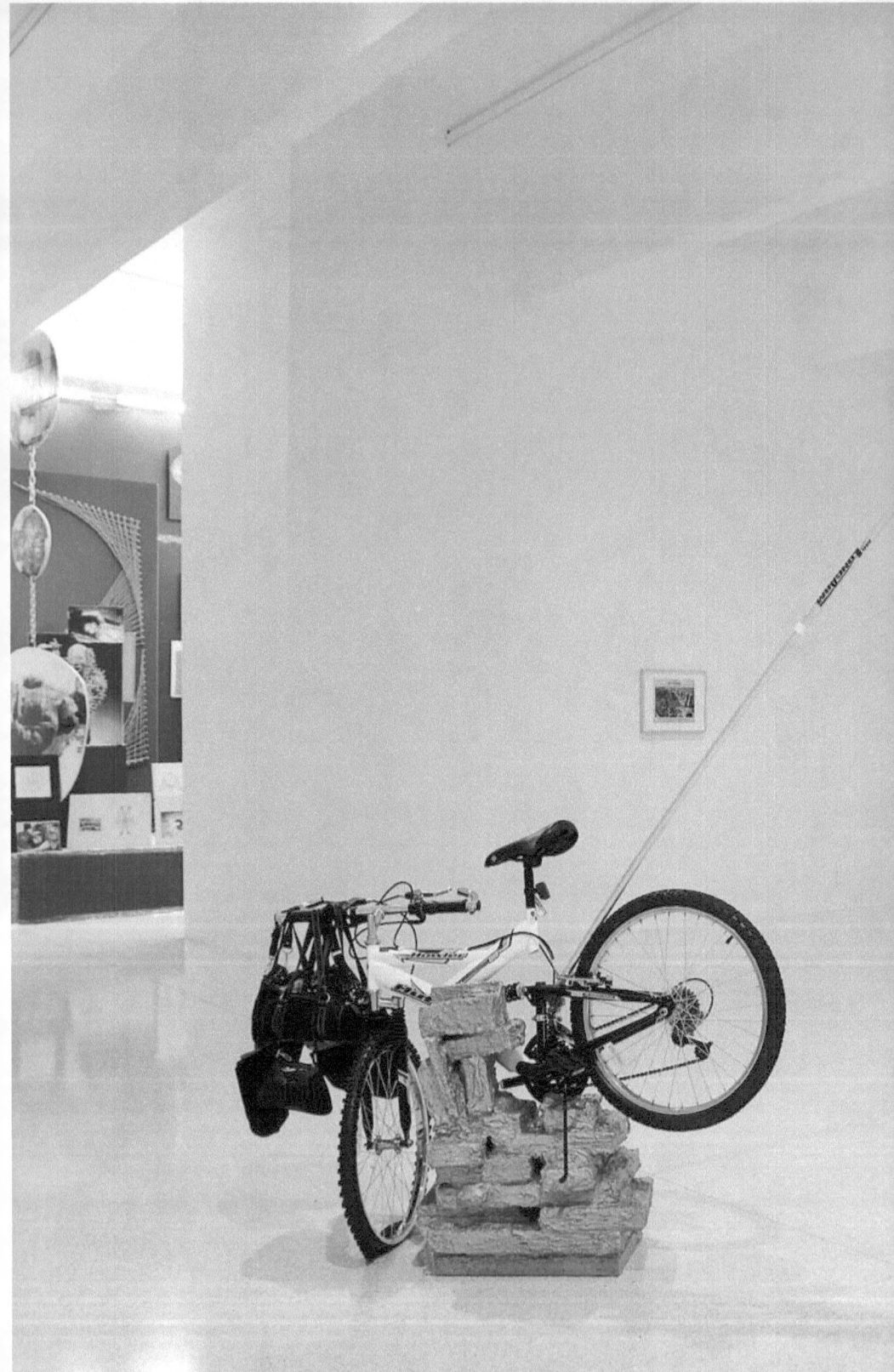

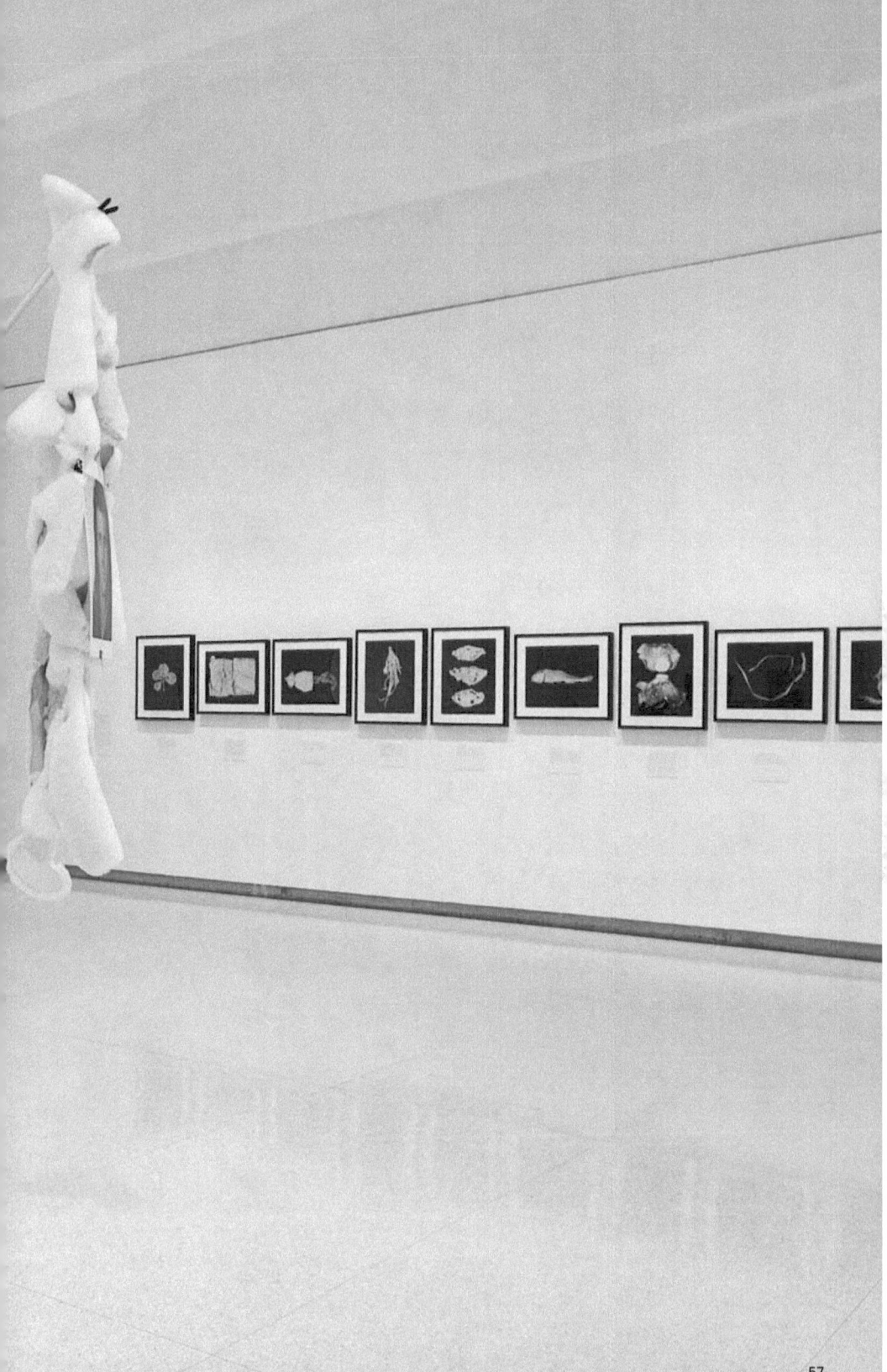

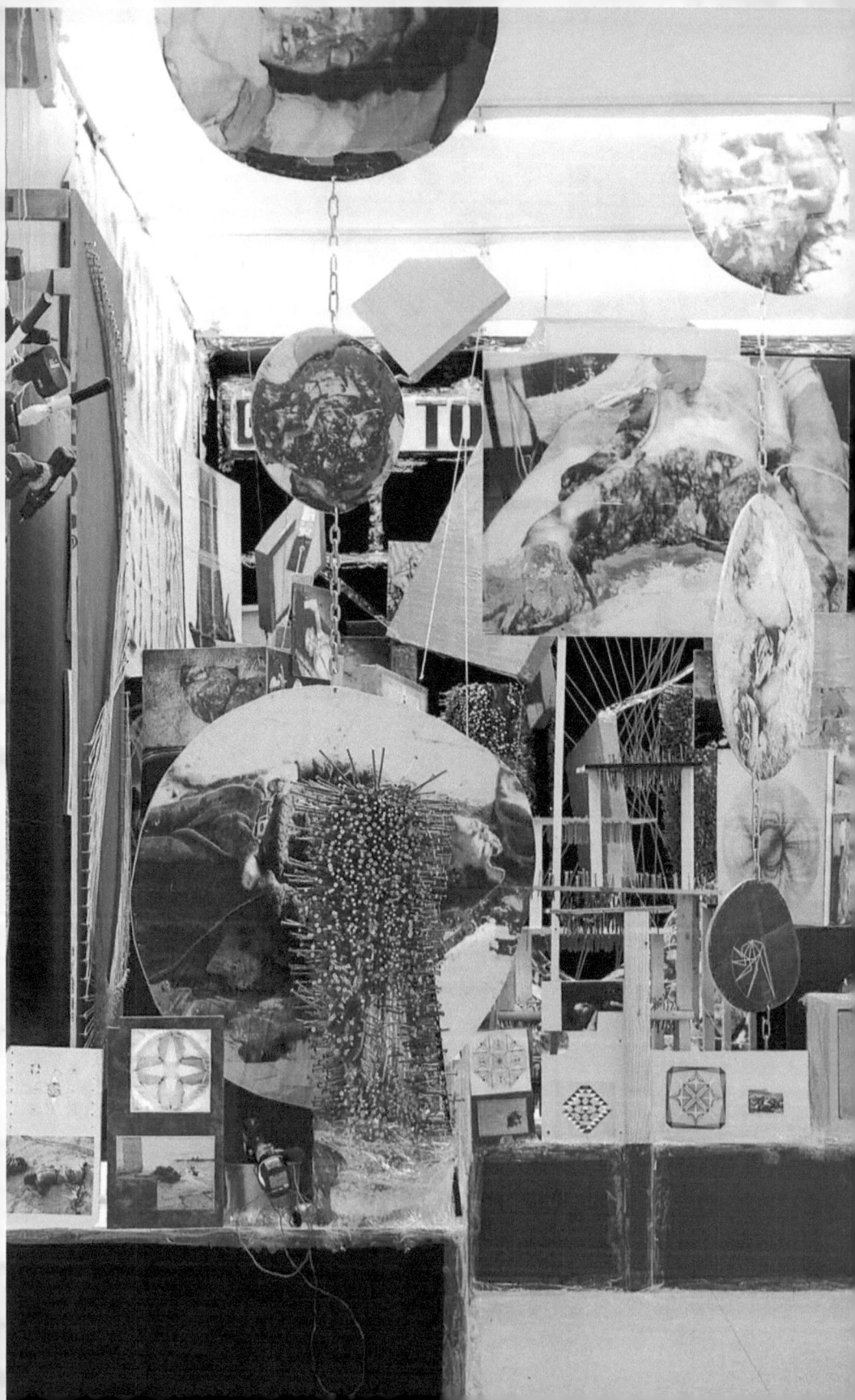

Simon Baier

Subject Matter

I. Anamnesis

With half-closed eyes, one could make out a faint haze.
Indistinct, luminous colors crystallize into forms, consolidate
into shapes, which at any moment loosen their contours again
and unravel into a swirl of tones. "A picture by Delacroix,"
Baudelaire suggests, "will already have quickened you with a
thrill of supernatural pleasure even if it be situated too far
away for you to be able to judge of its linear graces or the
more or less dramatic quality of its subject." Without the
delimiting virtue of lines, the image, whose subject dissolves
or might not even have appeared, is transformed into an immaterial sheen, whose actual place becomes difficult to pin down.
The wrong distance brings the image closer than it is: "You feel
as though a magical atmosphere has advanced towards you and
already envelops you." The suspension of the possibility to
judge—"une trop grande distance pour que vous puissiez juger"—
returns another type of evidence: "This impression"—an atmosphere, too far away and at the same time too close—"is certain
proof of the true, the perfect colourist." Lines divide the
ground, colors retreat within the boundaries of their assigned
contours. To approach the picture, to reach the point where it
closes itself off to a field—the point where a ground, a figure, and, at last, a subject (sujet) appear—all this does not
add anything. The pleasure Baudelaire speaks of does not need
any further cause. "And when you come closer and analyse the
subject, nothing will be deducted from, or added to, that original pleasure [plaisir primitif], for its source lies elsewhere
and far away from any material thought [pensée concrète]." It
is this evoked impression that "has taken its place once and for
all in your memory."[01] Vision, reduced to a somatic mode,
leaves an instantaneous, ineffaceable imprint: a memory and a
proof. This judgment—and there is no doubt that also here, as
in Kant, the type of pleasure Baudelaire speaks of is inextrica-
bly linked to a moment of judgment—is not only cut loose from
the reality of the thing that could be called its cause. It is
also, Baudelaire makes this very clear, independent from any

[01] Charles Baudelaire, "The Life and
Work of Eugène Delacroix" (1863), in
The Painter of Modern Life and
Other Essays, trans. and ed.
Jonathan Mayne (London: Phaidon,
1964), 51. For the original French
text, see Charles Baudelaire,
"L'œuvre et la vie de Eugène
Delacroix," in L'art romantique
(Paris: Louis Conard, 1917), 16.

representation. The impossibility to judge based on the absence
of concrete knowledge of a transferable content releases a force
of judgment, which has lost its ground.[02]

The focus on color introduced in the beginning (from too far
away) can be exchanged by coming closer (too close), to a point
where lines become the sole event to be seen. "So long as it is
skillfully drawn, there is nothing—from the limbs of a martyr
who is being flayed alive, to the body of a swooning nymph—that
does not admit of a kind of pleasure in whose elements the
subject-matter plays no part."[03] The exclusion of the subject
is absolute. In this respect the rhetoric of the text marks an
extreme, which, to be sure, cannot be said to be exemplary of
Baudelaire's thought, let alone Delacroix's. And yet the tropes
are no singular instances. Baudelaire repeats them, vehemently.
As a pleasure, it is totally alien and absolutely independent of
the depicted subject.

The image closes itself off from its referent to leave an
impression that one will never forget. One won't forget without
knowing, however, what it is. We will have to come back to this
point, which is, I feel, decisive. As a scene, it is a strangely
mechanistic setup. One should not forget that Baudelaire calls
Delacroix's paintings grandes machines[04]—machines for which
nature is reduced to a pure incitamentum,[05] an excitant. In
another instance, he even calls the visible universe fodder,
a form of pasture,[06] which imagination needs to digest, super-
imposing thus the organic with the mechanical. Minimized to an
excitant, the world gives way to a jouissance, which no swooning
is to disturb and no empathy with the depicted is to interrupt,
even if it might be flayed alive. The example of flaying is
intentionally drastic, and yet it is surely no question of morals
that is raised here. One revelation of pure flesh—the peeling
of skin in order to extract soma beyond form—is substituted for

[02] Kant writes: "On the other hand, the
judgment of taste is merely con-
templative; i.e., it is a judgment
which, indifferent as regards the
existence of an object, compares
its character with the feeling of
pleasure and pain." In this respect,
the aesthetic judgment yields
knowledge neither of the reality
outside the subject nor of the
subject itself. Since the actual
reality of the thing that gives
pleasure is put in parentheses, the
judgment can also not be described
in pathological terms, that is,
as mere mechanistic result of a
specific sensual stimulus (Immanuel
Kant, Critique of Judgment, trans.
J. H. Bernard [New York: Hafner,
1951], 43–44).
[03] Baudelaire, "Life and Work," 52;
Leo Steinberg cites this passage
in passing as an early example of
a model of formalist criticism.

Starting from there, my own reading
of the text aims to unpack what
specific implications Baudelaire's
sketch—which, as Steinberg rightly
notes, is not at all representative
of Baudelaire—might have for a
formalist theory and its complement,
abstract art. See Leo Steinberg,
"Other Criteria," in Other Criteria:
Confrontations with Twentieth-
Century Art (New York: Oxford
University Press, 1972), 64.
[04] Baudelaire, "L'œuvre et la vie," 4.
[05] Ibid., 15.
[06] Ibid., 12.
[07] "Glorifier le culte des images (ma
grande, mon unique, ma primitive
passion)" (Charles Baudelaire, "Mon
coeur mis à nu" [1909], 38.68, in
Journaux intimes [Paris: Librairie
José Corti, 1949], 94).
[08] Baudelaire, "Life and Work," 58.
[09] Ibid., 44.
[10] Steinberg, "Other Criteria," 64.

another pure impression. The evoked pleasure Baudelaire speaks
of is cut loose not only from the subject as represented. To a
certain extent it shows itself also beyond the control of the
beholding subject itself. Neither is left untouched. The impression has always already made its mark, a mark that remains
indiscernible to the subject. To withdraw, to distance oneself,
is therefore not enough. Painting beyond content demands a
sensation purified to an incisive thrill. It denotes what the
image on the forefront of a future of the senses is from now on
about. "To glorify the cult of images," this is what Baudelaire
programmatically identified as his "primitive passion."[07] It
is a cult whose interest, the surplus it yields, surpasses the
limits of passive intuition. Detachment and excitement are only
two sides of the same technique, which reduces the world to an
abstract image. This, maybe more than anything else, seems
to be the subtext of Baudelaire's eulogy, which outlines a
phenomenology of painting as effects. The subject, captured in a
paradoxical state in between calm restraint and nervous excitement, is thus mirrored in the description provided of Delacroix
himself: frail but "all energy, but energy which sprang from the
nerves," yet the remained hidden behind a "softening veil of
a civilized refinement." The "blinkings of concentration" made
his eyes appear small: "They seemed to do no more than sip at
the light."[08]

Slits through which only a fraction of the light passes, a
lack intensified to a flicker: flickering, iridescent canvases.
What is at stake, however, is not simply of psychophysiological
interest. It is not merely an analysis of seclusion and hyper-
aesthesia, phenomena pervasive in the aesthetic discourse at
the time, which retrospectively might sediment as pathology of
the bourgeois subject. And yet what Baudelaire describes is certainly not to be mistaken for mere fantasy, a projection based
on his own looking. It is, he contends, primarily a question of
composition. Composition transmits "the invisible, the impal-
pable, the dream, the nerves, the soul." As big as these claims
are, not only is what Baudelaire names vague, but he vacillates
between terms, which are neither exchangeable nor congruent. If
it seems far from clear what Delacroix has accomplished, the
means with which he has done it are not in question: "and this
he has done—allow me, please, to emphasize this point—with no
other means but colour and contour."[09]

For Baudelaire this fact is enough to distinguish him from
any other painter, not only of his time but also of the past.
The reduction to these essential elements of painting—which
seem to be its essence and distinguish it in its duality from
any other art—at the same time do not produce any exclusive
difference. The seemingly proto-formalist schema, which made Leo
Steinberg suggest placing it in a tradition that can be seen as
leading straight to Clement Greenberg,[10] does not result in the
essence of a medium. On the contrary, for Baudelaire, it opens

up the possibility of a heightened exchange among the arts. It is this strict reduction to the means of colors and lines that made, he contends, this art more accessible to poets than to painters. The unusual focus on purely abstract means (and, as we will see, Baudelaire will explicitly name it this way) is in fact not painterly. The turning away from subject matter does not lead painting to itself but rather opens it up toward language. And it is because of this that this painterly progress remained necessarily unseen by the painters of his time. What Delacroix's images transfer is therefore, even if it is unnameable, speech (parole).[11] We can therefore specify: if everything is done with no other means but color and contour, these colors nonetheless speak, the lines think. And yet what constitutes such a composition, a composition that, independent from any subject, incises the subject? Baudelaire's description of the world as a "store-house of images and signs," seems at first to imply that it is only a combination of already available things.[12] (He especially seems to tend to such a reading when he compares the work of the painter, who arranges colors like a bouquet of flowers, to that of a florist or even a window dresser.)[13] But the reduction to line and color goes much further than a mere appropriation and recombination: "Strictly speaking there is neither line nor color in nature....They are twin abstractions."[14] The fact that they are abstract puts color and line beyond the status of ready-made signs. The painter transfers a "pure excitant" (nature) to an objective abstraction. And yet this process is by no means clear. It implies at least a jump, as it crosses an unbridgeable rift. If color and contour don't exist in nature and yet become the sole basis of painting, any bond that might have tied nature and art is here severed. Any causality, any possible deduction from what subjectively excites to what is objectively composed in a block of sensation, is radically negated.[15] The repetitive insistence on the external quality of any thematic resemblance in the work of art can be understood only from this perspective. The creation of line and color, a creation that renounces nature as model, points to a place the work of art inhabits, in which ties to the world become precarious.

The proclaimed absence of line and color in nature exposes the work of art that makes them its sole basis to a situation in which any relation to the external world seems to be cut off. What is striking is that Baudelaire makes them operators that are not simply absent in the present. They also act against time. Not only do colors and lines speak, dream, and think something that cannot be seen on the canvas, but as moments that break world and artwork apart, they constitute at the very same time the material for what Baudelaire terms a mnemotechny.[16] Abstraction, and with it the pleasure evoked, converges with the problem of memory. They are, Baudelaire implies, inseparable. What could cautiously be called a theory of modern painting is based on this knot, in which these three elements intertwine.

What is to be remembered? And how is this to be done with contour and color alone? (Since this is, Baudelaire insists, what is <u>new</u> in Delacroix!) An abstract memory, maybe of nothing specific but—and might it be even precisely because of this?—ineffaceable. As far from Delacroix as Baudelaire's reading might be—and it is indisputable that it should not be mistaken for a close reading of any specific painting—one should not forget that—in all his hyperbole of subjects, in his strenuous hunt for the grand and dramatic—Delacroix's aim is to paint history. It is this unbearable task, which puts any failure in perspective, the failure to be true to a desire, which he acknowledged early on—"Je me suis senti un désir de peinture du siècle"[17]—as if this were a task painting could still fulfill. If there could be something like a painting of the century, one must be able to answer in turn the question of how the century could be painted. What Baudelaire casually calls the "more or less dramatic quality of the subject" is still to hold the tension to a will to depict the historical presence, or at least to become its symptom.[18] If Napoléon really was "the epopee of our century for all the arts," then it is striking that what remains of this "abundance of motifs"[19] in Delacroix's own oeuvre is nothing but two dead horses: <u>Le soir d'une bataille</u> (1845), a painting he made sketches for only one month after his musings. In 1814, on the heights between La Villette and Buttes-Chaumont, on the northern outskirts of Paris, where Delacroix found the motif for his sketches at a horse knacker, Marshal Marmont tried for the last time to hold off the Allies, a battle that marked the definitive end of the Napoleonic adventures.

This precise missing of the historical event, the belatedness on the side of content, which nonetheless harks back to the intended task—the depiction of an actual historical battle where now only a ghostly figure raises its head, as if climbing from a unknown dark where two dead horses melt with the human body to indistinct spots of white, gray, blue, and red, struggling to define themselves against a devouring field of black—is surely an exception in Delacroix's oeuvre. The flight to a dreamworld of orientalism marks the rule. Hubert Damisch is certainly right when he notes in his close reading of Delacroix's diaries that it is striking that, aside from <u>The Massacre at Chios</u> (1824) and <u>Liberty Leading the People</u> (1830), the artist did not seem very interested in the history of his century, despite his expressed

[11] Baudelaire, "L'œuvre et la vie," 3.
[12] Baudelaire, "Life and Work," 49.
[13] Ibid., 48.
[14] Ibid., 51.
[15] See Gilles Deleuze and Félix Guattari's notion of composition as a "block of sensation" in their <u>What Is Philosophy?</u> trans. Hugh Tomlinson and Graham Burchell (New York: Columbia University Press, 1996), 167.

[16] Baudelaire, "Life and Work," 45.
[17] <u>Journal de Eugène Delacroix</u>, vol. 1, <u>1822–1852</u> (Paris: Librairie Plon, 1932), 97 (May 9, 1824). Unless otherwise noted, all translations are by the author.
[18] Baudelaire, "Life and Work," 52.
[19] <u>Journal de Eugène Delacroix</u>, vol. 1, 99 (May 11, 1824).

desire. What Delacroix wanted cannot make disappear what brackets history, blocking it as a possible subject. Yet painting's anamnestic function, its ability to testify or even to constitute history, is not displaced, as Damisch at one point suggests, interpreting Delacroix's diaries as a specific ersatz for a memory that he sees unfulfilled in his paintings; nor is this anamnestic function simply given up.[20] How could this failure be compensated in the space of writing? And finally, how could this inability be removed from the space of the canvas?

If Baudelaire is right to speak of a new type of mnemotechny, a technique that inscribes beyond representation, without a thing to remember, it is a lack from which to start. (It is this lack, Damisch notes, this inability to even remember anything, that drove Delacroix to find prostheses, and his diary is surely one of them.)[21] Again, what should contour and color bring to mind? Baudelaire's answer is, as so often, embarrassingly direct: "the grandeur and the native passion of universal man."[22] One shouldn't dismiss this comment too quickly, a comment that oddly exudes the smell of abstraction as world language.[23] What is remembered is certainly no event. If anything, it is a mere possibility. Gestures (lines) and atmospheres (colors) transmit things that "one had believed to be forever buried in the dark night of the past."[24] Painting is not simply gestural. If it is at all expressive, it speaks in the past tense. Painting remembers gestures, a lost grandeur, that man no longer has, forever buried in the dark night of the past. If it is a universality of man, it is one of not having. It inscribes the failure to transmit: painting in the mode of spleen. If it is a glorification of the cult of images, it takes place in a state of vexation: Spleen and Ideal. Stefan George's proposed translation of the

---

[20] Damisch's reading of Delacroix's diaries sees the problem of mnemotechny deferred to in the relation between painting and writing. The diary becomes the stand-in for any project of mnemotechny that painting is no longer able to fulfill. Damisch writes, after referring to Baudelaire's hint at the problem of mnemotechny: "Le Journal lui servira donc d'aide-mémoire, et d'aide-mémoire, d'abord, pour la peinture" (Hubert Damisch, La peinture en écharpe: Delacroix, la photographie [Brussels: Yves Gevaert Éditeur, 2001], 31).

[21] See ibid.

[22] Baudelaire, "Life and Work," 45.

[23] The phrase "abstraction as world language" was introduced by Werner Haftmann, curator of Documenta II in 1959. Although he was certainly not the first to think about abstract art as an international force, his dictum marks a decisive moment when its internationalism was used in order to justify the current political order of the time. For evidence that such thinking is not simply a relic of the past, see Weltsprache Abstraktion: Gestalt, Magie und Zeichen, Museum Dahlem, Berlin, May 21–October 15, 2006.

[24] Baudelaire, "Life and Work," 45.

[25] The veil of tears as a screen in between the world and the subject, has, as Walter Benjamin showed, in Baudelaire's poems the paradigmatic function of such a mnemonic distortion. Through the veil, neither the presence nor a particular past can be seen, but what Benjamin termed Vorwelt, a world beyond history. See Walter Benjamin, "Über einige Motive bei Baudelaire," in Illuminationen: Ausgewählte Schriften, ed. Siegfried Unseld (Frankfurt am Main: Suhrkamp, 1961), 222.

[26] Charles Baudelaire, "Le public moderne et la photographie" (1859), in Curiosités esthétiques (Paris: Michel Calman Lévy, 1949), 258–59.

first word of this title for a collection of Baudelaire's poems as Trübsinn might point to a crucial connection. It hints not only at a certain mood but also at a register of sensual distortions: a clouding of the senses, in which memory from now on has its precarious place.[25]

There is, one cannot stop doubting, a fundamental inaccuracy at the core of this experience. One is even tempted to say that this is its specificity. To call it abstraction asks for a chronology. When does it take place? After the painting is made? As abstraction, it surely has no pictorial style; it is faceless, unidentifiable in its appearance. It does not even reach the level of production. Its image will have been abstracted. Yet despite its precision of composition, it is certainly not introduced as timeless perfection. Its timelessness is tied to modernity. Its acting against time is fettered to progress. It is forced to compete with a cult of sun worshippers, of fanatics, narcissists, with an ignorant mass audience, following the voice of a vengeful god into the desert of reproducibility, with Daguerre as their messiah.[26] In Baudelaire's schema it is photography that figures as painting's dangerous misleader. It is a struggle of beliefs, and it is far from accidental that Baudelaire deploys the same characteristics—the nomenclature of sects, heresies, of a base, pathological iconophilic religiosity—when he describes his own counter-project of painting. The two cults are dangerously close. Even for Baudelaire it is no secure flight of painting to a domain that it could properly call its own. If we can speak of resistance, painting fights in the same mode as the tendency that it opposes. Painting, which aims to condense the world to an abstract dream image, has its doppelgänger in the image industries of photography and film. Its strategy of abstraction is a resistance to another one, and it can easily be seen how it is caught in between complicity and reaction. In all its unwilling cunning, Baudelaire's dialectics repetitively heads for this oscillating point of indistinction.

To be sure, his diatribes against photography should teach one the opposite. As paradigmatic symptom of modern technique and industrialization, he masks it, in a text of 1859 titled "Photography and the Modern Public," as art's polar opposite. The whole text exudes the desperate need for a hygiene that could separate the field of artistic practice from any contamination by its industrialized context, in which photography has to figure as the epitome of materialist progress, a force that, it seems, is able to eradicate poetry and art tout court. What is conjured is a state of technical materiality, in which the flight of spirit is complete, leaving nothing more for the subject than to simply register what has been recorded. As an opposition it forces Baudelaire to ascribe to art the most ineffable attributes: the immaterial, the ethereal, the original, the spiritual, and above all fantasy. All this, photography, he contends, by its very nature is able neither to provide nor to emulate: "When industry breaks into the domain of art, it inevitably has to become its deadly enemy. The mixing up of their functions leads to a point where none of them can be ful- filled."[27] But how to disentangle their functions at a histori- cal moment when they are already fused? (Baudelaire's enmity is proof of this.) In order to secure art any place of its own, he ascribes it one in which it has lost all material reality. The radical opposition of industrial technique, embodied through photography, leaves art empty-handed, secluded to a realm where it cannot actualize itself anymore as part of modern society: a surplus value without capital.

If the mixing up of industry and art leads to a condition where neither can be fulfilled, the project to separate the two faces the same dilemma. Whereas the concrete existence within an industrialized world appears to block art's actual potential, its purification prohibits its realization. Baudelaire's proposed synthesis within this double bind is feudal: industrial tech- nique as art's servant, a slave that does nothing but produce and a master that does nothing but enjoy. Art's immaterializa- tion, its identification as a fantasy, becomes the mere logical result of its being in a world that it does not produce but, as he thinks, that it could still transform through consumption alone: a subjugation of industry to artistry, through which the first is to be completely altered by the latter.[28] If this is to mean more than a mere hiding of existing relations, if it is to mean an overcoming of modernity through the work of art, it is, to be sure, as utopian as the projection of the purely economic- industrial domain that is about to threaten it.

Note how Baudelaire, already four years earlier, in one of his articles on the Exposition Universelle of 1855 in Paris, where Delacroix's paintings, a group of them even, were exhibit- ed as well, acknowledged how the aesthetic domain most success- fully invaded the realm of industry, when he admires an imported commodity from China as "a sample of universal beauty."[29] It is this very beauty, which is rapidly about to question the distinctions between aesthetics and the economic-industrial complex, that is widely staging its unforeseeable powers in the ever newly invented display structures of gigantic world expositions. Moreover, the very means of artistry are supplied

[27] Ibid., 261
[28] Ibid.
[29] Charles Baudelaire, "Exposition Universelle de 1855" (1855), in Curiosités esthétiques, 212. Giorgio Agamben comments extensively on this passage in Stanzas: Word and Phantasm in Western Culture (Minneapolis: University of Minnesota Press, 1993), 41.
[30] Baudelaire, "L'œuvre et la vie," 10.
[31] Paul Signac, D'Eugène Delacroix au néo-impressionnisme (Paris: Floury, 1939).

[32] Cited in Alain Badiou, The Century, trans. Alberto Toscano (Cambridge, England, and Malden, Mass.: Polity, 2006), 57.
[33] The paradoxical endpoint of the abstract work of art, which cuts off any reference to anything outside itself in order to become absolutely autonomous, is its logical exposition to its own contextual conditions as a material object.

by industry, even if art is done at home, with brush and paint alone. The question of whether art sells or not only touches the surface of the problem. It is above all its aesthetic reception that is reciprocally modeled on its own economic appropriation.

What has been termed the commodification of art marks maybe above all the reimport of the aesthetization of the commodity into the field of the aesthetic itself. It therefore concerns not merely art's being for sale but, at a more fundamental level, the mode of its reception, the desire it elicits, the desire for a prize, and the gaze it asks for. How can artistic production materially intervene in this scene where the subtleties of a new type of beauty reign, long before anything enters the exhibition space? If there is anything produced, it is combined and adjusted through montage "avec un certain art."[30] Since what art is, and what its production specifies, has become too unspecific to pin down, there can no longer be any mode of artistic production proper. This is the lesson of the deadlock Baudelaire so forcefully pursued. The barred place within industrial production places it on the forefront of a mode that pretends to create through modes of consumption alone. Artistic production is already here no longer a skill proper, a way of doing and making, which essentially transforms matter, but one that collects and accumulates. Maybe more than a work of destruction or of waste, the artwork becomes a halting point of incessant, aimless accretion, in which the artist as producer is assimilating himself to the side of the consumer. It is because of this that Paul Signac can retrospectively describe Delacroix's achievement as one of color contrasts solely, a tonal progress, realized through a placement of distinct, unmixed brushstrokes, a heightening of sensation through disjunct tâches.[31]

II. Amnesia

This all takes place long before the aim to depict is triumphantly let go, long before a new reality of the work of art is announced, which self-sufficiently is to actualize what until now has remained implicit. It is a history for which abstraction, in its utopian dream of forgetting, has no need. Now the past is to be eradicated in anticipation of a horizonless future to come: to "erase the bygone days," as Malevich put it in one of his poems.[32] It's not simply that the history of making art is to be cut in two but that the space of the work itself is no longer to be a container of an accumulated, narrated time. By freezing over the mnemonic depth of the window of the picture plane, its other-timeliness is reduced to a continuous now, the now of nonrepresentation, through which in turn the integrity of the artwork's difference is exposed to the contextual changes of its surroundings.[33] Against the repetitive insistence of things past, it is to affirm the repetitive presence of the new. The radical materiality proposed has its complement in the purity of a sight beyond bodily finitude. With the erasure of the horizontal separation of the picture plane, as Malevich announced,[34] a separation that distinguishes up and down, earth and sky, as a last remnant to orient the viewer in an earthlike simulation space, an eye beyond any perspectival limit is dreamt, that is, beyond the limit inherited by the subject as being in the world, before it even projects its first gaze: a wordless eye.

Viewed from this narrow height, it is a short century of abstraction. And it is far from clear where exactly its pure style is to be located, untainted by the limits of its own history. This is how abstract art presents itself to us: one style among many available to choose from. As historically closed ism, which cannot simply be taken up and continued, it has become the cipher of an unrealized modernity whose muteness makes it foreign as well as universally applicable. As a nonexclusive solution whose actual telos appears implausible to pursue, it persists as a mere shade, as hue or grade within the spectrum of present possible image productions. As such a look, abstraction has become in itself mere material for a much more abstract machine, one that values and devalues every object as image and, in turn, every image as object: an anonymous machine that assigns shelf lives for any visibility and its ever-new moment to come. The precarious historical moment of abstract art seems thus to be lost in its own prehistory and forever after, two halves that mirror each other as they refer to an axis, which in itself can no longer be seen. Abstraction's dream of forgetting has, so it seems, befallen abstract art itself, whose intention appears ungraspable to the present. Its historical moment has become the object of a process that does not allow us to situate it as a thing to remember but makes it oscillate as an immediately disposable form, one whose time seems neither gone nor come.

"Before there was an art of abstract painting, it was already widely believed that the value of a picture was a matter of colors and shapes alone."[35] The rift is sewed, and a genealogy is laid out in an instant. This is how "The Nature of Abstract Art" (1937), Meyer Schapiro's revision of the historical

[34] To "step out of the ring of the horizon" has become one of the most famous proclamations of Malevich's nonobjectivity (Kazimir Malevich, "From Cubism and Futurism to Suprematism: The New Realism in Painting" [1914], in Essays on Art, 1915–1933, ed. Troels Andersen, trans. Xenia Glowacki-Prus and Arnold McMillin, vol. 1 [London: Rapp & Whiting, 1969]).

[35] Meyer Schapiro, "Nature of Abstract Art" (1937), in Modern Art: Nineteenth and Twentieth Centuries: Selected Papers (New York: G. Braziller, 1978), 185.

[36] Ibid.

[37] For the reception and influence of the German art historical tradition on Russian formalism, see in particular the chapter "The Formal Method in European Art Scholarship," in Pavel N. Medvedev, The Formal Method in Literary Scholarship: A Critical Introduction to Sociological Poetics (1928; Baltimore and London: Johns Hopkins University Press, 1991), 41–52.

[38] Schapiro, "Nature of Abstract Art," 185.

[39] Ibid., 187, 196; see Alfred H. Barr Jr., Cubism and Abstract Art (New York: Museum of Modern Art, 1936).

breakthrough of abstraction, starts out. It perhaps marks—
against the doubt, still persisting at the time, over whether
to accept abstraction within the art historical pantheon—one
of the earliest efforts to reduce it to a mere style. As a
manifest style, Schapiro notes, it makes visible only what
has long since been the substratum governing any judgment on
pictures: "Abstract art had therefore the value of a practical
demonstration."[36] One value is measured against another: the
value of a practical demonstration against the universal value
of pictures. One cannot reformulate modernity's flight out of
time more drily. Surely there has been formalism, as it was
conceptualized within the German art historical tradition of
the late nineteenth and early twentieth centuries, which could
be said to have discursively facilitated an appreciation and
acceptance of abstract art before the fact.[37] And it is certainly mainly this art historical tradition that Schapiro is
pointing to. Yet the inferences reach much further. Abstract
art is not to be seen primarily as a leap into the future, as
Malevich contends. If anything, Schapiro implies, one should
speak of a particular belatedness.

Schapiro's essay sets a tone, far removed from the euphoric
or utopian mood that accompanied the announced breaking of mimetic chains only twenty years earlier. Malevich's, Mondrian's,
even Kandinsky's progressive thrust is drowned in cautious
skepticism, which inevitably dissolves the radical difference
of abstraction in a faceless historical continuum. (And it is
drowned, one might add, before a second rehearsal of the hege-
mony of abstraction after the Second World War is attempted.)
If the practical demonstration of abstraction makes manifest
what has been latent, it may not simply be a revelation but
should in itself be analyzed as a particular mode of disguise.
Schapiro's comment is to be read word for word: "In abstract
art, however, the pretended autonomy and absoluteness of the
aesthetic emerged in a concrete form. Here, finally, was an art
of painting in which only aesthetic elements seem to be present."[38] The manifestation of the latent pretends an absoluteness
of the aesthetic, which only seems to be present. A new reference, a semantic operation of representation, is at work, which
points to itself in order to hide its actual genesis. Abstraction is a form of illusion that presents itself as an event in
which all masks seem to have been dropped and the real is to be
encountered. Or, to phrase it in more traditional terms, the
ideology of abstraction is to picture itself as an absolute
concrete form: a form nonetheless.

Referring to his main target of criticism, Alfred H. Barr's
catalogue for the seminal exhibition Cubism and Abstract Art,
presented at the Museum of Modern Art in 1936, Schapiro con-
cludes that, as a form, abstraction is not absolute but is a
"language of absolutes." It symbolizes—and it speaks. It speaks
of an art "unconditioned by experience."[39] Abstraction is not

only belated, considering how any image is governed by its
particular mode of reception, an ability to confer value based
on colors and shapes alone. Schapiro feels, opposing Clement
Greenberg before he even starts to write, that a purely affirmative outlook on abstract art and its underlying assumption—
the universal progress of global reason, identified with the
advanced industrial-economic complex—is impossible to maintain
in the already-looming shadow of the Second World War, in which
the coldest monster, called the nation-state, will industrial-
ize the systematic killing of millions. No solemnly floating
circles and squares: another silence. If anything is to appear,
it should be "empty spaces, bones, grotesque beings, abandoned
buildings and catastrophic earth formations."[40] There is an
experience that underlies the reception of any image, but there
is also on the side of the artist the experience of a world,
which makes it plausible to abstract from it. Schapiro charac-
terizes here almost word for word what Greenberg is later to
denounce as "gothic" tendencies: a return of Surrealism and
Dada in the wake of a questioning of a progress of universal
history, at which endpoint the inevitability of purely abstract
painting stood.

Empty spaces, bones, grotesque beings, abandoned buildings,
and catastrophic earth formations: these are not only the
worldly outcomes of a side of abstraction whose force left
nothing untouched. As remnants of a world whose ghostly contours
reappear on the surface of the picture plane, they can neither
be thought nor seen without their former disappearance. The
pulse of figuration has lost any force to initiate a return to
order. What reappears is a figure under conditions according
to which a work of art is no longer to represent anything.
Or to be more precise, if it has ever been absent, it reappears
when the very term representation has lost any distinctive force
against its opposite. "The ideas underlying abstract art have
penetrated deeply into all artistic theory, even of their original opponents....The language of absolutes and pure sources
of art, whether of feeling, reason, intuition or the sub-con-
scious mind, appears in the very schools which renounce abstraction."[41] Schapiro's leveling of abstraction to a style is not
aimed only at its ideological underpinnings. At least here he
does not argue for a return to a more humane face of art. Much
more, he seems to imply that the situation has come to a point
where it is no longer decisive to distinguish between abstraction and its opposition in order to make a mark. In this context
what should be called the return of the repressed, the figure or
its dissolution, the mimetic impulse or its negation? And again,
what in fact could be a more adequate response to the state of
the world? The affirmative repetition of effacements in the
name of absolutes or the farcical attempt to trace the singular
instance of events, in the language of a commodified object of
financial speculation.

Languages and ideas. This is how abstraction penetrates into art, which speaks in a language of absolutes. And it is again languages and ideas that are to renounce the unrenounceable since it has penetrated too deeply, again, not into praxis, but into theory. Nothing, it seems, is really done or made here, but thought through, even though it appears to be a thought that does not come to an end. What returns is a disfigurement. Bones and grotesque beings are its mere symbols. The belatedness the text is pointing to seems due to a specific belatedness that has befallen art itself, a belatedness that enables it to speak only in ideological terms. This is no idealist missing of praxis, but the acknowledgment that it is art's very praxis that is in itself becoming theoretical. Or, in order to return to what we tried to analyze earlier with the help of Baudelaire: it does not even reach the level of production. On the contrary, it is production that has become the phantasm of abstraction, pointing to that which is real but can neither be seen nor taken over. The wide belief that abstract art is making manifest, a belief that is able to confer value on a picture and that is able to anchor this value in the presence of colors and shapes alone, points not to an eradication of figures in order to reveal an empty screen. What abstraction as a process within artistic production points to might not be the ban of reference but the reverse, its initiated infinity. The promised gain is set as the outcome of a split within the subject itself, whose felt sensation is worth more than the evoked image.[42] Or in return: the evoked image has become nothing else than its contraction to pure sensation. It might not be accidental that the term belief, used by Schapiro, echoes the cult of Baudelaire. It is precisely here where economization and imagination intertwine and a pure substratum of the image as investment is extracted. It entails not the subject's eradication but the objectless investment: an exploitation of phantasms. The disfiguration of the representational regime pushes the image to the edge of an absolute presentness whose mnemonic dimension becomes a vacancy that the work of art displays as a historic medium, produced beyond its historic time.

[40] Schapiro, "Nature of Abstract Art," 211.
[41] Ibid., 187.
[42] "La sensation éprouvable vaut plus que son image suggérée" (Pierre Klossowski, La monnaie vivante [Paris: Editions Losfeld, 1994], 21).

«Concrete Shock» ① →

Aubervilliers 13. Februar
2006. Liebe Sabine,
ich will hier versuchen
in ein paar Sätzen fest-
zuhalten was los war in
New York mit meiner
Ausstellung «Superficial
Engagement». Die Aus-
stellung ist nun, nach nur
fünf Wochen beendet und
wird heute Montag, abgebaut. Ich bin überrascht, einmal mehr,
über die Reaktionen zu meiner Arbeit. Die Besucher waren
zum Teil schockiert und vorallem verstört. Sie waren verstört
weil ich in meiner Arbeit Photos zum Teil durch Photokopien
vergrössert zeige von explodierten, zerstückelten, zerstörten
Körpern von Menschen. Es ging mir nicht darum tote Menschen
zu zeigen sondern die absurde Zerstörung des menschlichen Körpers
seit Afghanistan, Irak 9/11 London Suizid-Bombers Bali Israel etc.
Wissen wir wie das aussieht. Auf ~~~~ Internet-sites kann man
jeden Tag die neuesten Bilder sehen. Es geht nicht mehr ums
töten, um den Tod es geht um Zerstörung. Kürzlich erreicht
das Abbild eines ~~~~ zerfetzten Opfers eines Attentats oder
das Abbild des sich in die Luft gesprengten Attentäters ein
Grad der Abstraktion der über das was selbst
das Vorstellungsvermögen begreifen kann
hinausgeht. Ich wollte diesen Grad
von Abstraktion konfrontieren mit dem Grad abstrakter
Grad der Abstraktion von Kunst. Ich Kunst
wollte das was an der Oberfläche das Ver-
bindende ist sich miteinander konfrontieren
lassen. Deshalb der Titel der Ausstellung:
«Superficial Engagement». Ich wollte
eine Ausstellung machen die mit Bildern aus
der mich umgebenden Welt von heute
über die Fakten hinausgeht. Es geht mir
nicht darum: wer ist Opfer? wer ist Täter?
Wer ist Dominierender? wer ist Unterworfener?

Aubervilliers, February 13, 2006

Dear Sabine,

I want to try here to record in just a few
sentences what happened in New York at my
exhibition Superficial Engagement. The exhibition has now ended after five weeks and will
be disassembled today, Monday. I am, once again,
surprised by the reactions to my work. The
visitors were partly shocked and above all
disturbed. They were disturbed because in my
work I show photos—some enlarged by photocopy-
ing—of exploded, dismembered, destroyed human
bodies. My concern was not to show dead people
but to show the absurd destruction of human
bodies from Afghanistan, Iraq, 9/11, London
suicide bombers, Bali, Israel, etc. We do know
what that looks like! On websites we can see
the latest images every day. It is no longer
about killing, about death; it is about destruction. For me, the image of a mangled victim of
a bomb attack or the image of a suicide bomber
reaches a degree of abstraction way beyond what
we can conceive with our imagination. I wanted
to confront this degree of abstraction with
the degree of abstraction of Art, of abstract
Art. I wanted the different connections on the
surface to confront one another. Therefore the
title of the exhibition, Superficial Engagement.
I wanted to make an exhibition that reaches
beyond facts, with images from the world around
me today. For me it is not a matter of: Who
is the victim? Who is the culprit or the
perpetrator? Who is the oppressor? Who is the
oppressed or the subjugated?

Wer ist im „Recht"? Wer ist im „Unrecht"? Wer ist Gewinner? Wer ist Verlierer? Es geht mir darum anhand von Bildern aus der Welt in der ich lebe, denn es gibt nur eine Welt - aufzuzeigen Was meine Position ist, wo ich stehe, was ich - als Künstler-will"! Ich denke, dass Kunst - als Kunst die Kraft hat zu heilen! ~~~~~~~~ Kunst besitzt dieses Absolute, das die alltäglichen Denkschemas und Fakten- information durchbrechen kann. Kunst besitzt die Energie, über das heraus- zu gehen Was uns in der ~~~~~ politischen, kulturellen, ökonomischen, religiösen und sozialen Fakten- gläubigkeit versucht, zu kontrollieren, einzuschüchtern und schluss- endlich Hoffnungslos zu machen! ~~~~~~~~

Ich denke es gibt Kräfte und Stärken, die eine Sprengkraft besitzen, die über das „Realistische" hinausgehen. Um aber dieses „Realistische Denken" zu erschüttern muss ich mich - mit meiner Arbeit selbst an der Realität messen, Sie konfrontieren, Ich muss es doch wagen mich mit der Realität zu konfrontieren, ja, mit ihr zu co-operieren, um etwas zu verändern! Ich muss es doch riskieren, den Anderen zu beeinflussen ohne ihn neutralisieren zu wollen! Das habe ich versucht. Das habe ich auch erreicht, zumindest teilweise. Und natürlich ist es nicht das erste Mal, dass „Widerstand" stattfindet: diese Missverständnisse, dieses Gefühl bei vielen, ich wolle provo- zieren und schockieren diese Reaktionen bei denen eine totale Hilflosigkeit und Verlorenheit sich offenbart, Ja, es geht nicht darum, in der Kunst, die Indifferenz zu unterstützen oder die Gleichgültigkeit zu fördern! Aber mir geht es hie darum etwas „Problematisches" zu machen!

Who is in the "right"? Who is in the "wrong"?
Who is the winner? Who is the loser? For me it
is a matter of showing, by using images from the
world in which I live—because there is only one
world—what my position is, where I stand, what
I want to achieve as an artist! I think that
Art, as Art, has the power to heal! Art possesses this absoluteness that can break through
the everyday frame of thought and factual information. Art possesses the energy to go beyond
that which in the political, cultural, economic,
religious, and social belief in facts tries
to control us, to intimidate us, and ultimately
to make us lose hope! I think that there are
forces and strengths that have an explosive
power that goes beyond the "realistic." In
order to disrupt this "realistic thinking," I
must, however—through my work—measure myself
with this reality and confront it. I must risk
myself to confront reality—yes, indeed—and
even cooperate with it, in order to change
something! I must risk touching the other without wanting to neutralize him or her. That is
what I have tried to do. I have achieved this,
at least in part, and of course it is not the
first time that there has been a "resistance":
these misunderstandings, this feeling that many
people had that I wanted to provoke and shock,
these are reactions revealing a total helpless-
ness and lack of orientation. Indeed, in Art,
the point is certainly not about supporting or
promoting indifference! But I am not concerned
with "problematizing" something!

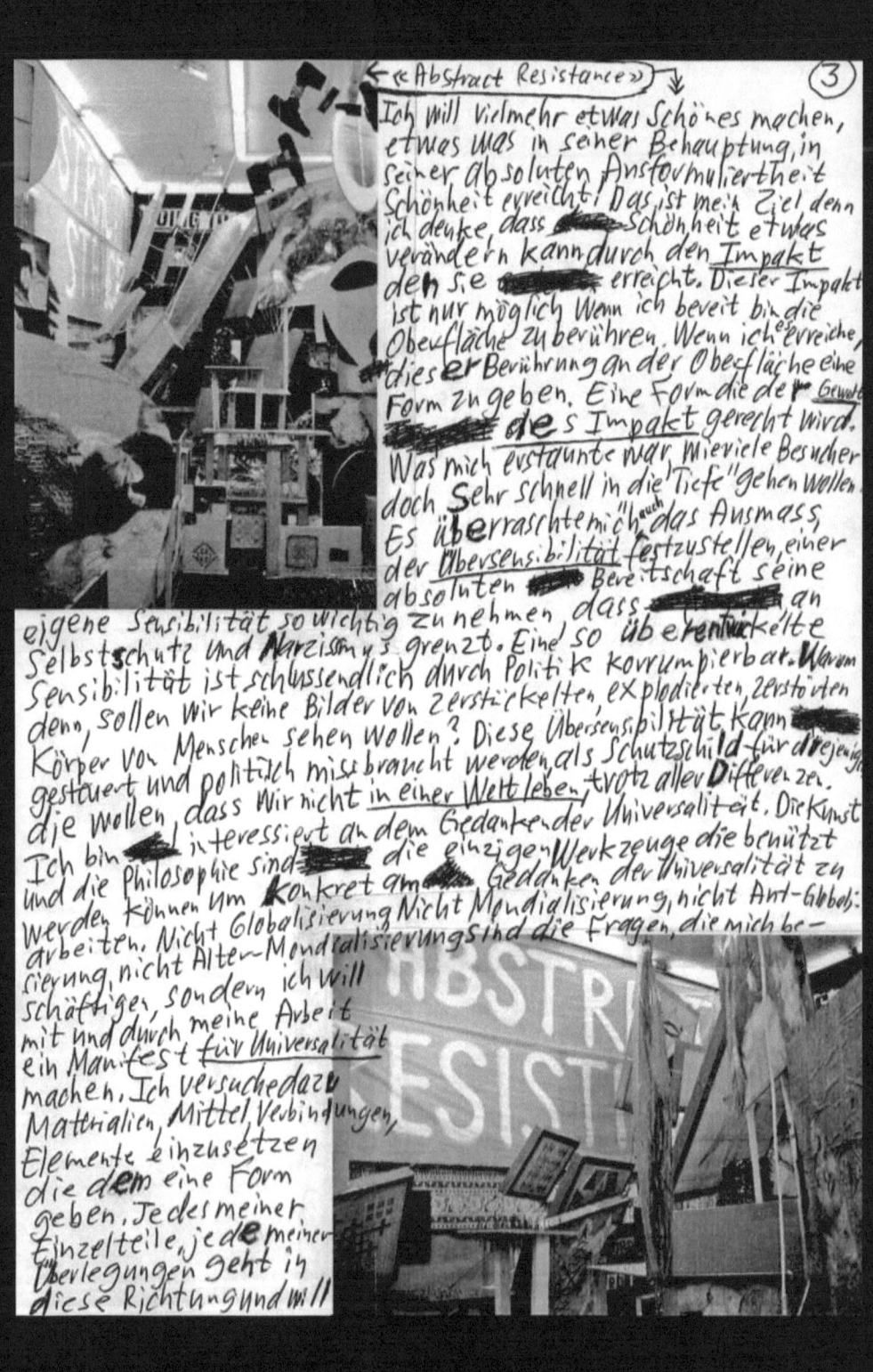

Ich will vielmehr etwas Schönes machen, etwas was in seiner Behauptung, in seiner absoluten Ausformuliertheit Schönheit erreicht. Das ist mein Ziel denn ich denke, dass ~~die~~ Schönheit etwas verändern kann durch den Impakt den sie ~~~~ erreicht. Dieser Impakt ist nur möglich wenn ich bereit bin die Oberfläche zu berühren. Wenn ich erreiche, diese Berührung an der Oberfläche eine Form zu geben. Eine Form die der ~~Gewalt~~ ~~~~ des Impakt gerecht wird.

Was mich erstaunte war, wieviele Besucher doch sehr schnell in die "Tiefe" gehen wollen. Es überraschte mich auch das Ausmass, der Übersensibilität festzustellen, einer absoluten ~~~~ Bereitschaft seine eigene Sensibilität so wichtig zu nehmen dass ~~~~ an Selbstschutz und Narzissmus grenzt. Eine so überentwickelte Sensibilität ist schlussendlich durch Politik korrumpierbar. Warum denn, sollen wir keine Bilder von zerstückelten, explodierten, zerstörten Körper von Menschen sehen wollen? Diese Übersensibilität kann ~~~~ gesteuert und politisch missbraucht werden als Schutzschild für diejenige die wollen, dass wir nicht in einer Welt leben, trotz aller Differenzen.

Ich bin ~~~~ interessiert an dem Gedanke der Universalität. Die Kunst und die Philosophie sind ~~~~ die einzigen Werkzeuge die benützt werden können um konkret am ~~~~ Gedanken der Universalität zu arbeiten. Nicht Globalisierung, Nicht Mondialisierung, nicht Ant-Globalisierung, nicht Alter-Mondialisierung sind die Fragen, die mich beschäftigen, sondern ich will meine Arbeit mit und durch meine Arbeit ein Manifest ~~für~~ Universalität machen. Ich versuche dazu Materialien, Mittel Verbindungen, Elemente einzusetzen die dem eine Form geben. Jedes meiner Einzelteile, jede meiner Überlegungen geht in diese Richtung und will

Rather, I want to make something beautiful, something that—in its assertion, in its absolute detailed formulation—achieves beauty! That is my aim because I think that beauty can change something through the impact it attains. This impact is possible only if I am prepared to touch the surface, if I succeed in giving a form to this touching of the surface, a form that is appropriate to the force of the impact. What amazed me was just how many visitors wanted to go quickly into the "depths." I was also surprised by the degree of hypersensitivity, by an absolute readiness to consider one's own sensibilities as so important, to the point of self-protection and narcissism. Such an overly refined sensibility is ultimately open to being corrupted by politics. Why, then, should we not want to see any images of dismembered, exploded, destroyed bodies of human beings? This hypersensitivity can be controlled and abused politically as a protective shield for those who want us not to live in the one world, despite all differences. I am interested in the thought of universality. Art and Philosophy are the only tools that can be used to work concretely on the thought of universality. My concern is not globalization, not antiglobalization, not alternative globalization, but rather to make, with and through my work, a manifesto for universality. In order to do this, I try to employ the materials, means, connections, elements that give this thought a form. Each of my individual works, each of my thoughts, follows this direction and wants to live up to this ambition.

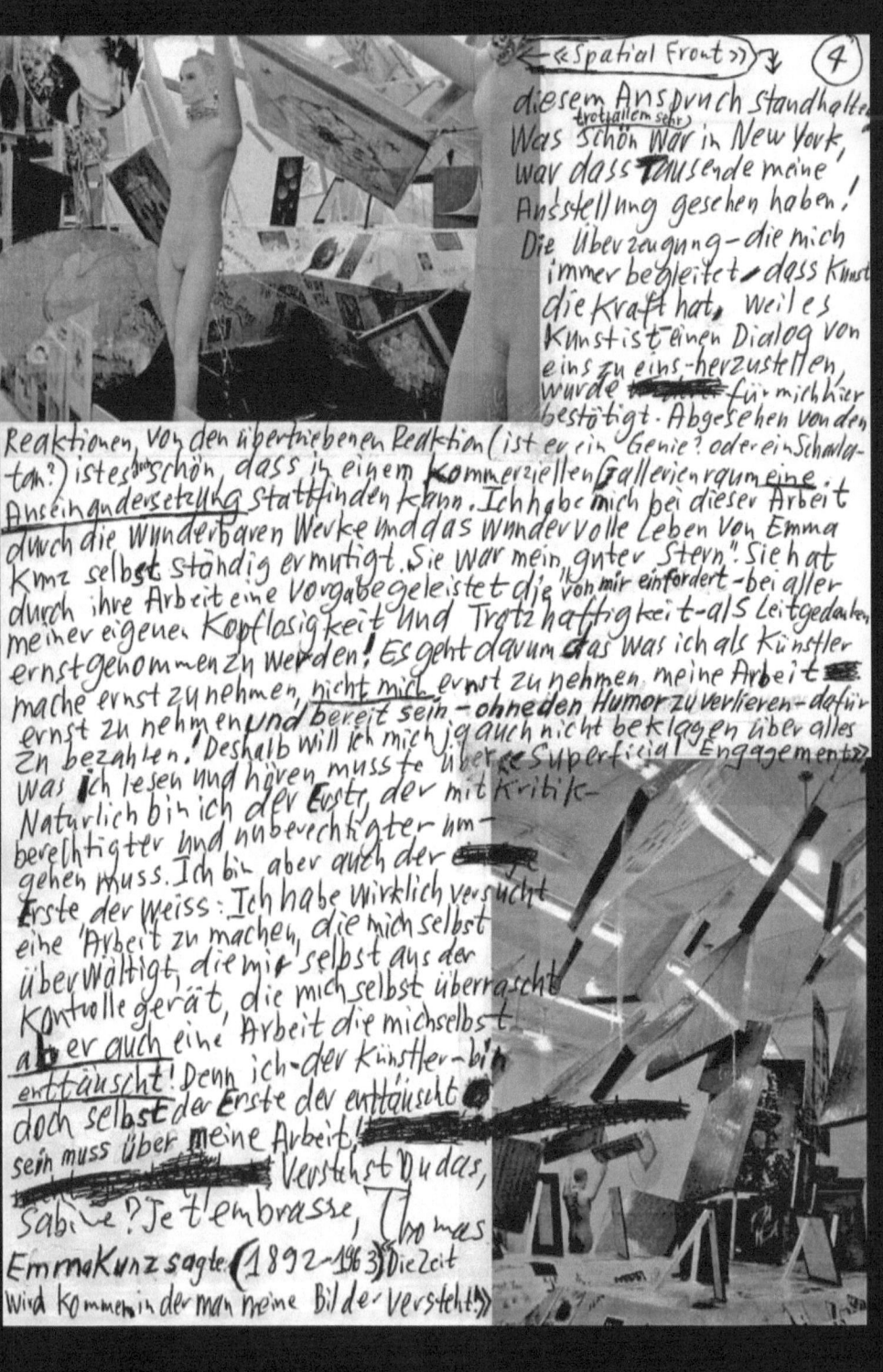

diesem Anspruch standhalten (trotz allem sehr)
Was schön war in New York,
war dass Tausende meine
Ausstellung gesehen haben!
Die Überzeugung - die mich
immer begleitet, dass Kunst
die Kraft hat, weil es
Kunst ist - einen Dialog von
eins zu eins, - herzustellen,
wurde ~~~~ für mich hier
bestätigt. Abgesehen von den
Reaktionen, von den übertriebenen Reaktion (ist er ein Genie? oder ein Scharla-
tan?) ist es auch schön, dass in einem kommerziellen Gallerienraum eine
Auseinandersetzung stattfinden kann. Ich habe mich bei dieser Arbeit
durch die wunderbaren Werke und das wundervolle Leben von Emma
Kunz selbst ständig ermutigt. Sie war mein "guter Stern". Sie hat
durch ihre Arbeit eine Vorgabe geleistet die von mir einfordert - bei aller
meiner eigenen Kopflosigkeit und Trotzhaftigkeit - als Leitgedanke
ernst genommen zu werden! Es geht darum das was ich als Künstler
mache ernst zu nehmen, nicht mich ernst zu nehmen, meine Arbeit ~~~
ernst zu nehmen und bereit sein - ohne den Humor zu verlieren - dafür
zu bezahlen! Deshalb will ich mich ja auch nicht beklagen über alles
was ich lesen und hören musste über «Superficial Engagement»
Natürlich bin ich der Erste, der mit Kritik -
berechtigter und unberechtigter - um-
gehen muss. Ich bin aber auch der ~~~
Erste der weiss: Ich habe wirklich versucht
eine Arbeit zu machen, die mich selbst
überwältigt, die mir selbst aus der
Kontrolle gerät, die mich selbst überrascht
aber auch eine Arbeit die mich selbst
enttäuscht! Denn ich - der Künstler - bin
doch selbst der Erste der enttäuscht
sein muss über meine Arbeit!
~~~~~ Verstehst Du das,
Sabine? Je t'embrasse, Thomas
Emma Kunz sagte (1892-1963) Die Zeit
wird kommen in der man meine Bilder versteht!»

The nice thing in New York, despite everything, was that thousands of people saw my exhibition! The belief, which I always have in mind, that Art has the force, because it is Art, to create a one-on-one dialogue was here confirmed. Apart from the reactions, the exaggerated reactions— is he a genius? or a charlatan?—the nice thing was that a critical, engaged discussion could take place in a commercial gallery space. As I was working, the beautiful works and the wonderful life of Emma Kunz constantly encouraged me. She was my "guiding star." With her work she achieved something exemplary that, as a guiding thought and despite all my own headlessness and refractoriness, demanded to be taken seriously! It means to take seriously what I do as an artist, not to take myself seriously, but to take my work seriously and be prepared, without losing my sense of humor, to pay the price for it! Therefore I won't complain about all I read and heard about Superficial Engagement. Of course, I am the first one to deal with justified and unjustified criticism. I am, however, also the first one who knows: I have really tried to make a work that overpowers me, that escapes my own control, that surprises me, but also a work that disappoints me! For I, the artist, am the first one who has to be disappointed by my work! Do you understand that, Sabine?

Je t'embrasse,
Thomas

Emma Kunz (1892–1963) said, "The time will come when people will understand my paintings."

Translated from the German by Michael Eldred, Cologne

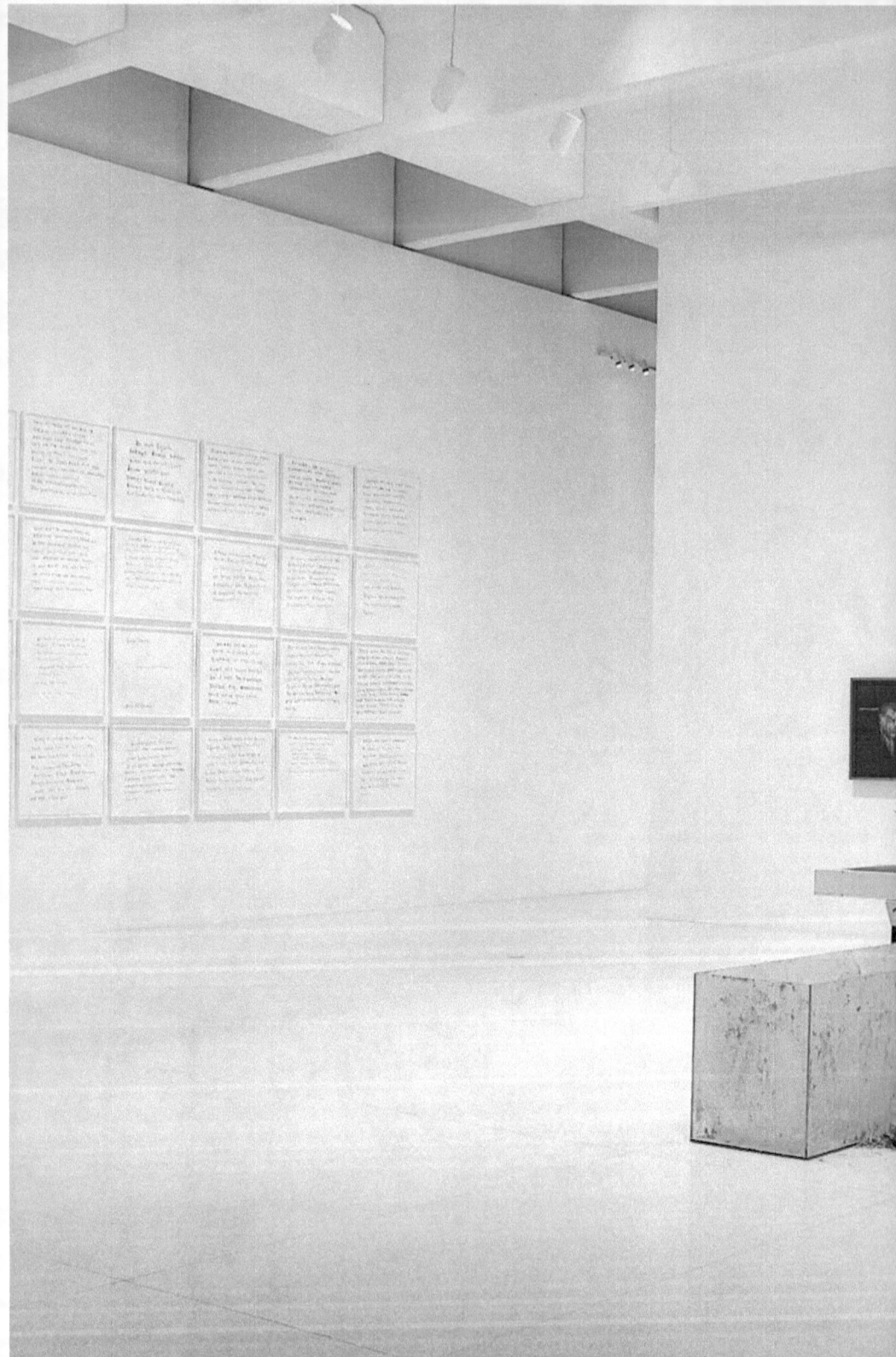

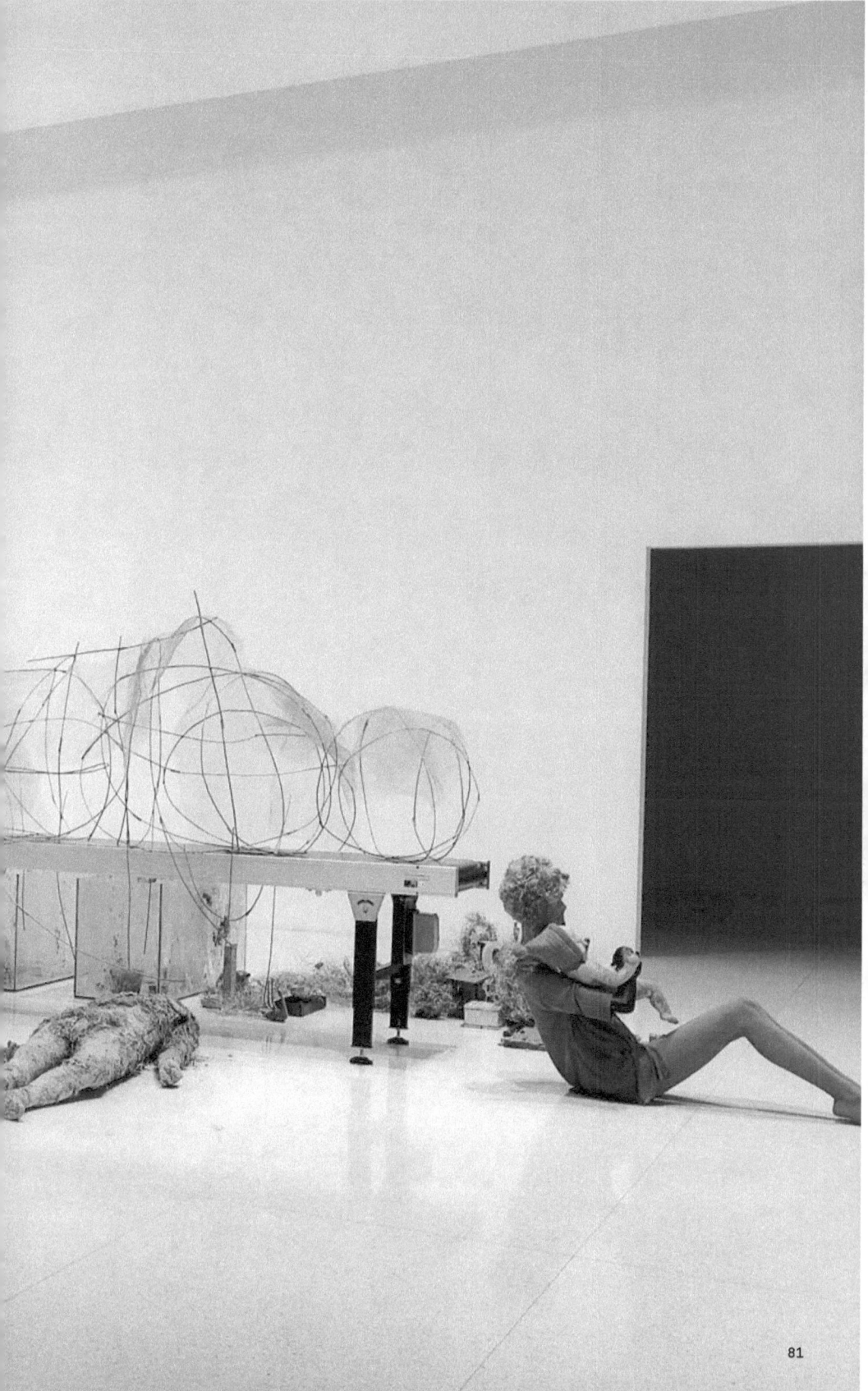

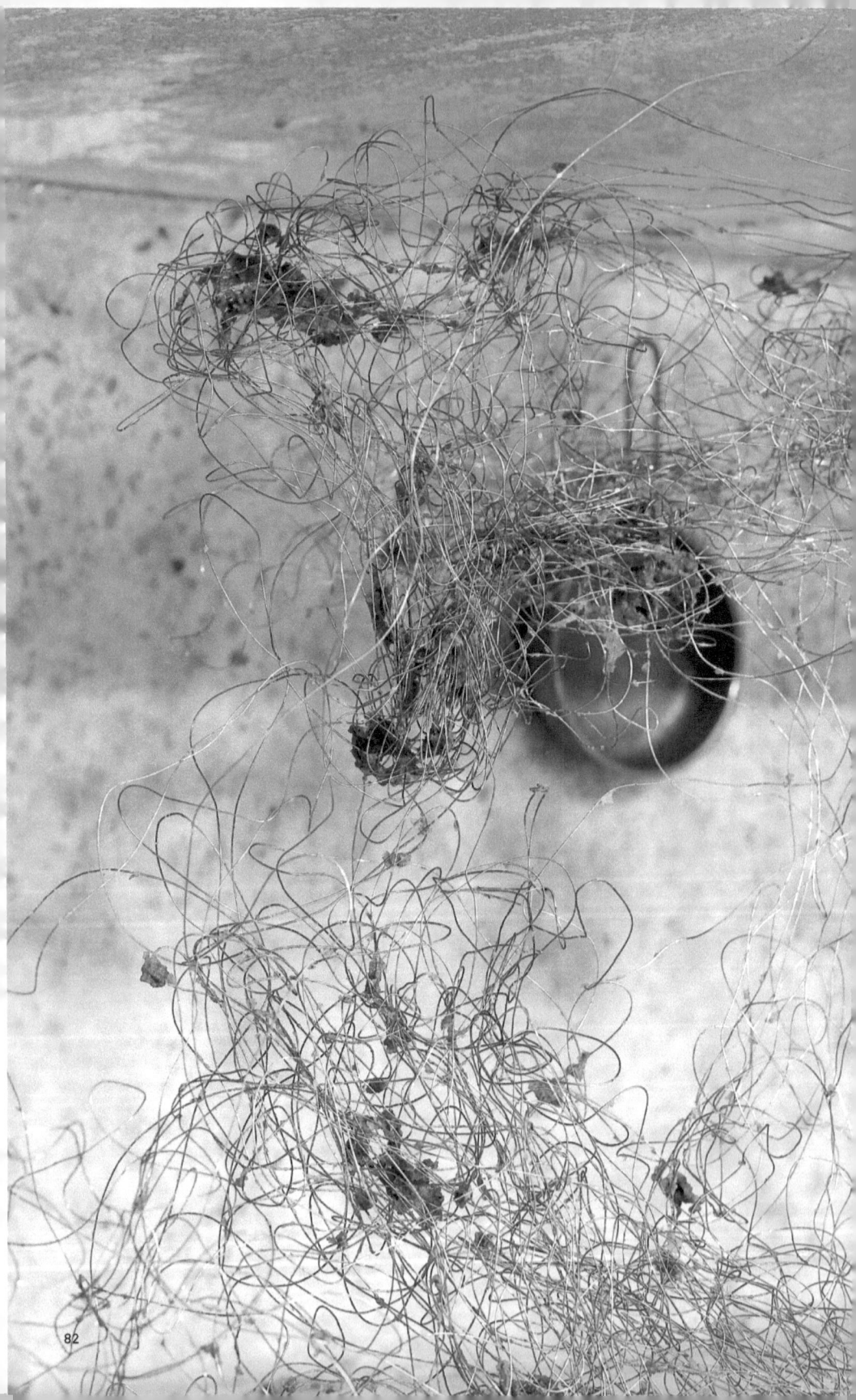

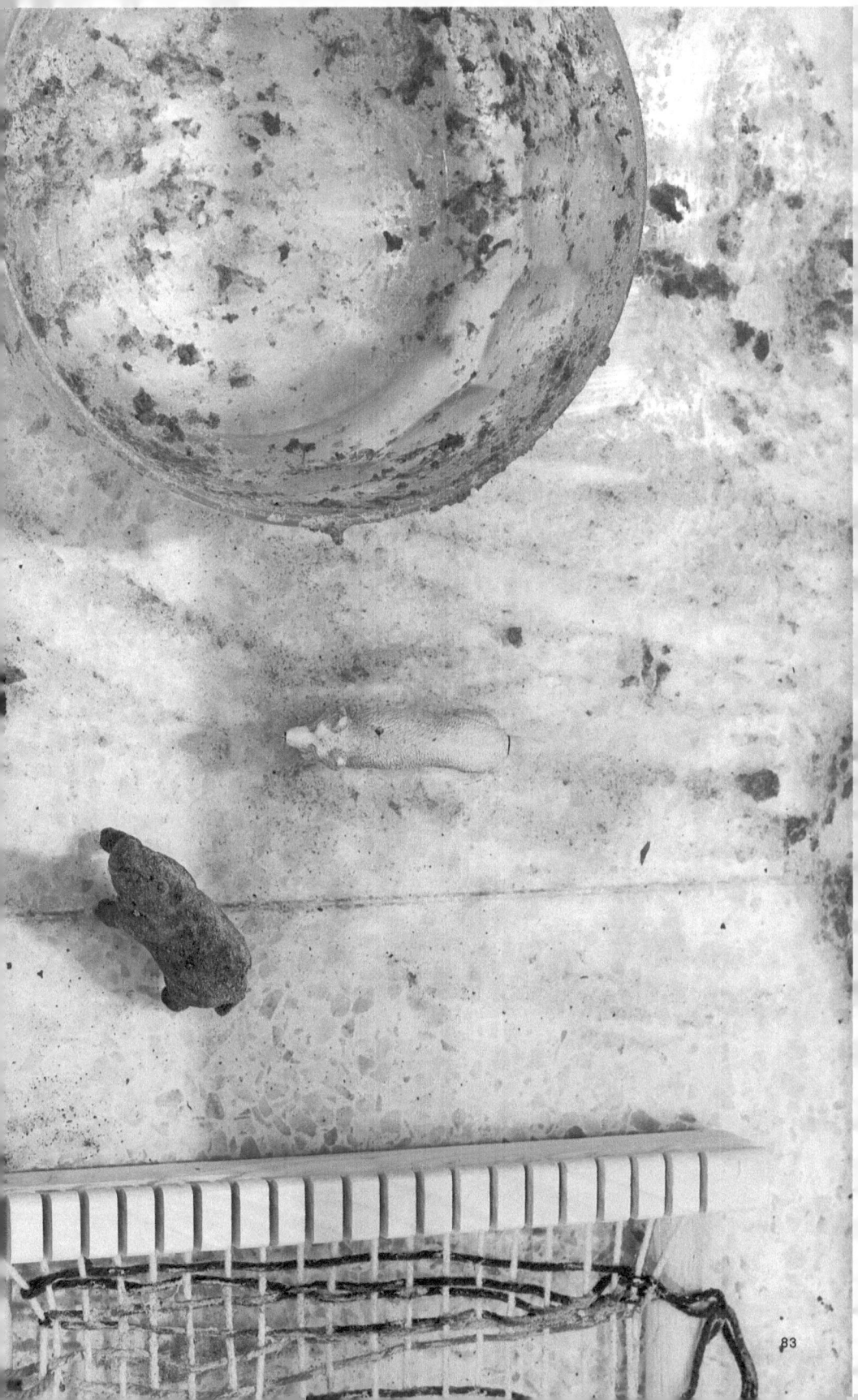

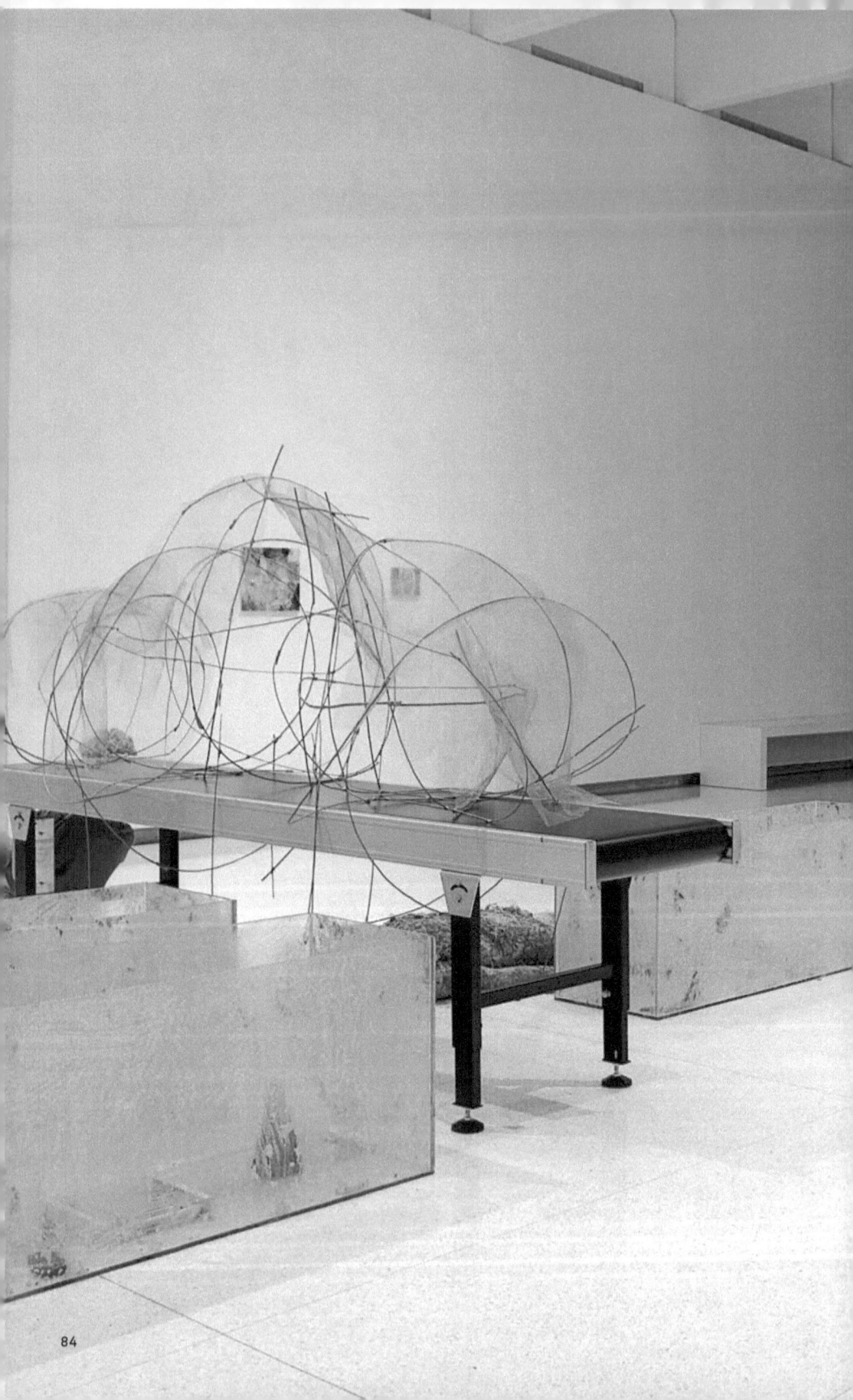

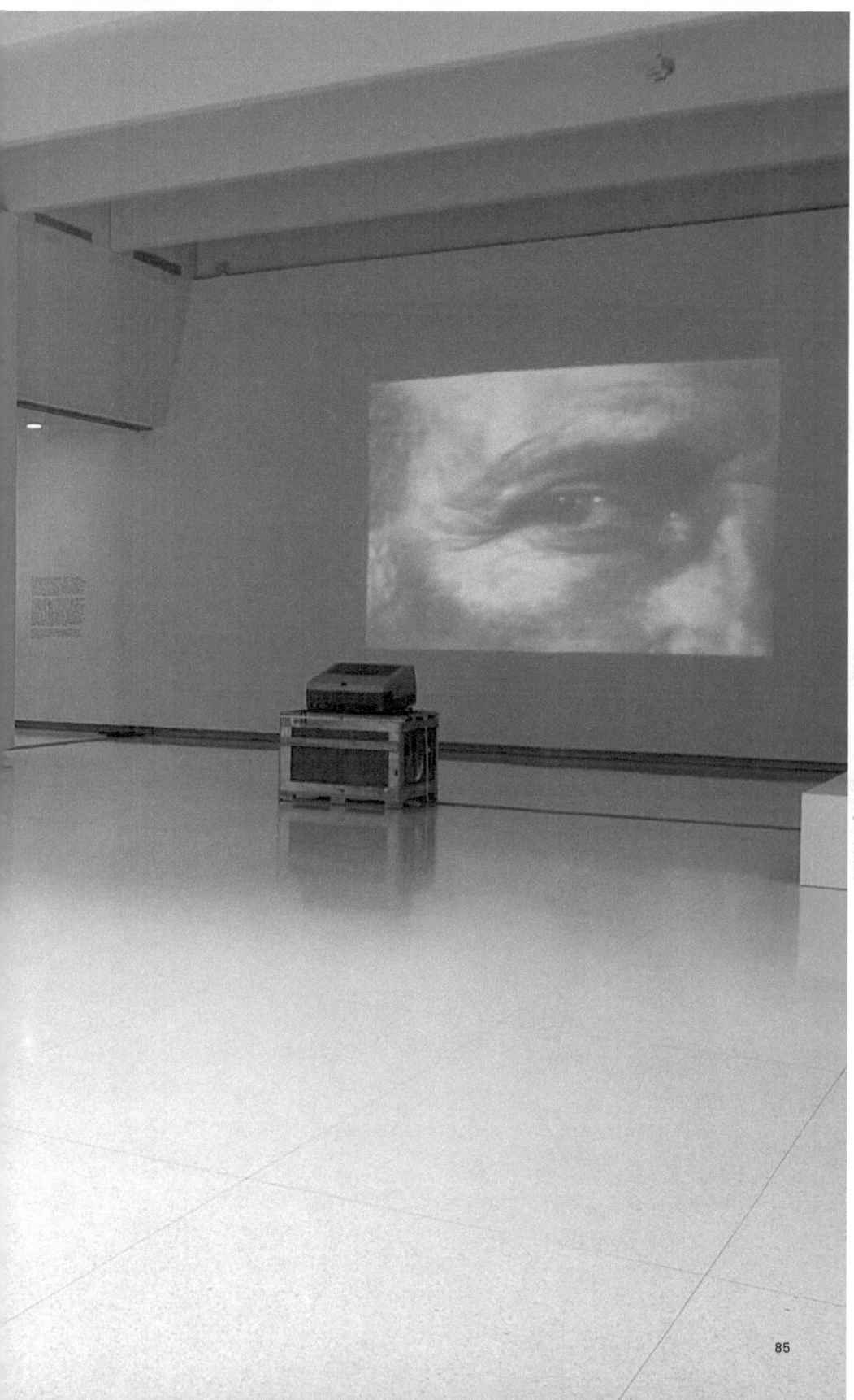

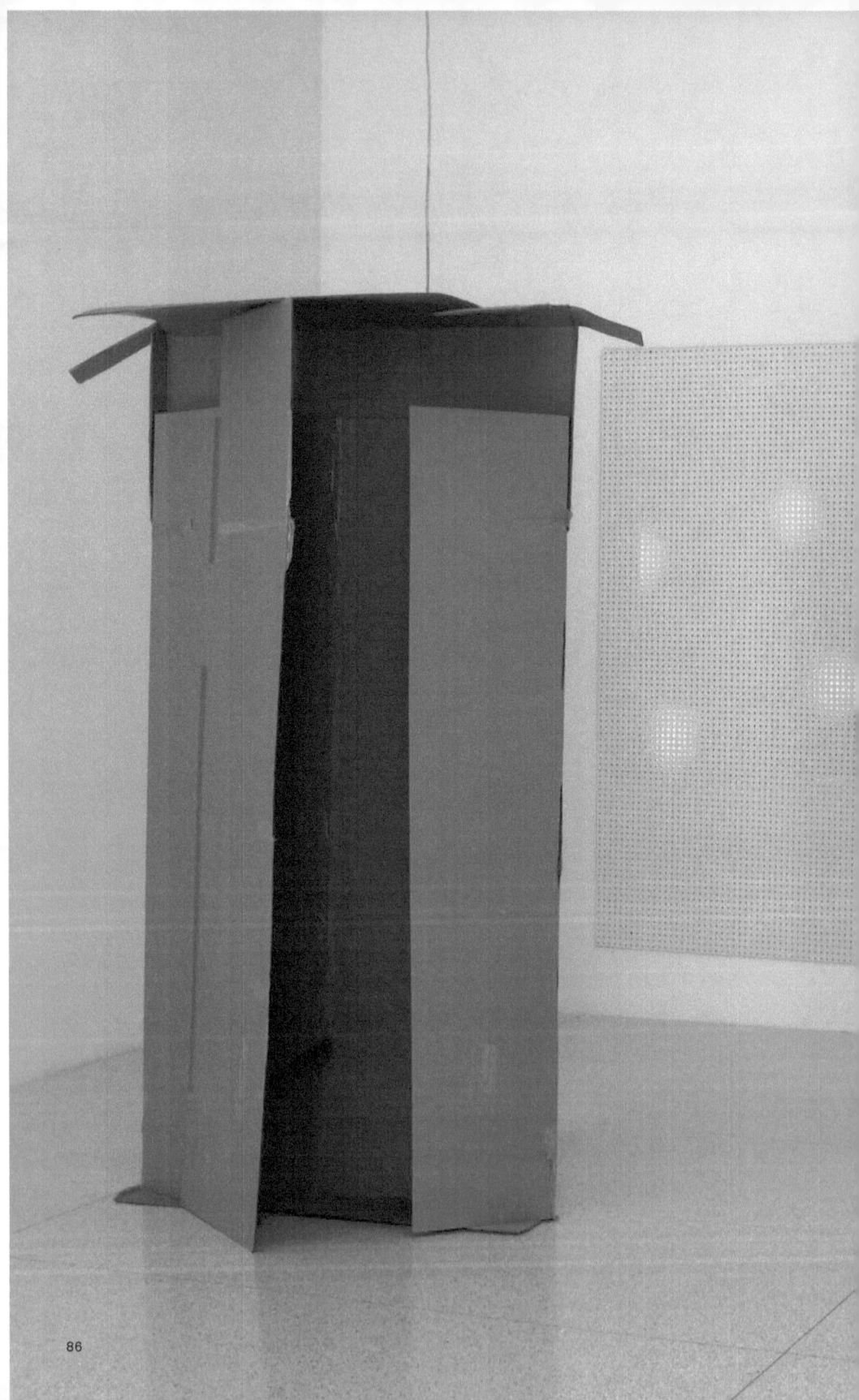

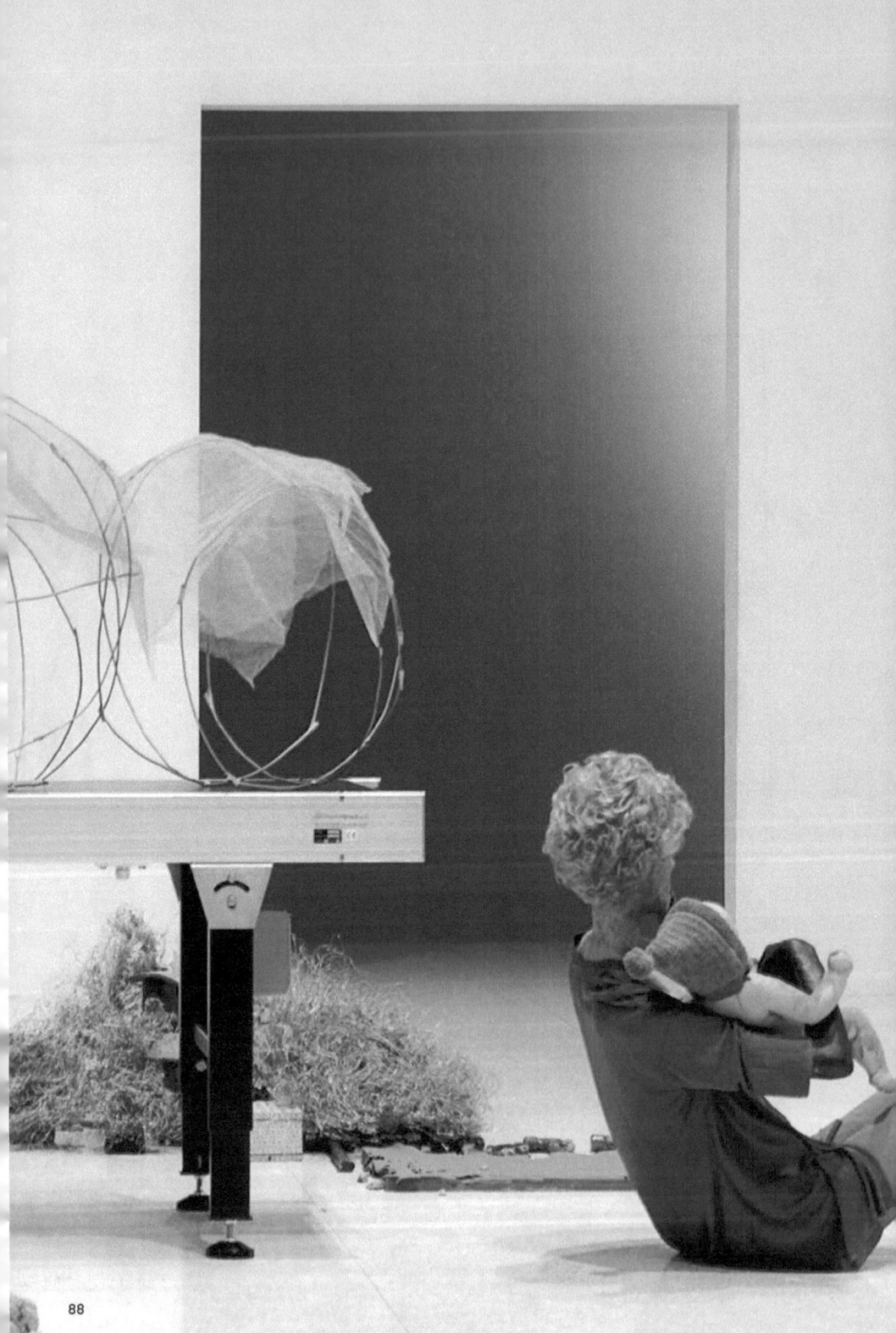

Exhibition Checklist

Unless otherwise noted, works in the exhibition are Collection Walker Art Center, Minneapolis.

FRANCIS BACON Irish, 1909–1992
Head in Grey 1955
oil on canvas
24⅛ x 20⅛ x ½ in.
(61.3 x 51.1 x 1.3 cm)
Donated by Mr. and Mrs. Edmond R. Ruben, 1995

LYNDA BENGLIS American, b. 1941
Element from Adhesive Products 1971
pigment, polyurethane
80 x 36 x 12 in.
(203.2 x 91.4 x 30.5 cm)
Acquired in conjunction with the exhibition New Work for New Spaces, original artwork composed of 10 elements, 1997

Excess 1971
purified beeswax, damar resin, pigments on Masonite and wood
36 x 5 x 4 in.
(91.4 x 12.7 x 10.2 cm)
Art Center Acquisition Fund, 1972

ANTHONY CARO British, b. 1924
Sculpture Three, 1962 1962
steel, paint, aluminum
78⁸⁄₁₆ x 62⁷⁄₈ x 148⁵⁄₈ in.
(199.4 x 159.7 x 377.5 cm)
Gift of the T. B. Walker Foundation, 1967

SARAH CHARLESWORTH American, b. 1947
April 21, 1978 from Modern History 1978
45 black-and-white direct-positive prints
dimensions variable
Justin Smith Purchase Fund, 2003

BRUCE CONNER American, 1933–2008
RATBASTARD 1958
wood, canvas, nylon, newspaper, photo-graphic reproduction, wire, oil paint, nails, bead chain, etc.
16½ x 9¼ x 2¾ in.
(41.9 x 23.5 x 7 cm)
Gift of Lannan Foundation, 1997

RATBASTARD 2 1958
wood, nylon, twine, candle, glass marbles, paint, nutshells, photograph-ic reproduction, metal charm, string, feather, sequins
20½ x 10³⁄₁₆ x 2¹⁄₁₆ in.
(52.1 x 25.9 x 5.2 cm)
Gift of Lannan Foundation, 1997

THE BRIDE 1960
wood, nylon, string, wax, paint, candles, costume jewelry, marbles, paper doily, etc.
36½ x 17 x 23 in.
(92.7 x 43.2 x 58.4 cm)
Braunstein/Quay Gallery and T. B. Walker Acquisition Fund, 1987

UNTITLED, FEBRUARY 4 1960
wood, Masonite, feathers, nylon, broken mirror, silk, lace, cotton, tin, wire, plastic bead, engraving collage on paper
17 x 14½ x 6¾ in.
(43.2 x 36.8 x 17.1 cm)
Gift of Lannan Foundation, 1997

SON OF THE SHEIK 1963
nylon stocking, nylon, beads, lace, dried grass, plastic, seeds, string, twine, wood, paint, fur, etc.
on Masonite
66 x 22 x 9¼ in.
(167.6 x 55.9 x 23.5 cm)
Gift of Lannan Foundation, 1997

WILLEM DE KOONING American, b. Netherlands, 1904–1997
Woman circa 1952
pastel, graphite on paper
13½ x 10⁵⁄₁₆ in.
(34.3 x 26.2 cm)
Donated by Mr. and Mrs. Edmond R. Ruben, 1995

LUCIO FONTANA Italian, b. Argentina, 1899–1968
Concetto Spaziale (Spatial Concept) 1958
perforations, graphite on paper
13 x 9½ in.
(33 x 24.1 cm)
Miriam and Erwin Kelen Acquisition Fund for Drawings, 1995

Concetto Spaziale–Attesa (Spatial Concept–Expectation) 1964–1965
tempera on canvas, lacquered wood
57½ x 45 in. (146.1 x 114.3 cm)
T. B. Walker Acquisition Fund, 1998

HOLLIS FRAMPTON   American, 1936–1984
(nostalgia)   1971
16mm film (black and white, sound);
36 minutes
Ruben/Bentson Film/Video
Study Collection, Walker Art Center
Courtesy The Estate of Hollis
Frampton and Anthology Film Archives,
New York City

Untitled I-XIV from ADSVMVS ABSVMVS   1982
14 Ektacolor photographs on resin-coated
paper
20 x 16 in.
(50.8 x 40.6 cm) each
Clinton and Della Walker Acquisition
Fund, 1993

PHILIP GUSTON   American, 1913–1980
Bombay   1976
oil on canvas
78 x 114½ x 1 in.
(198.1 x 290.8 x 2.5 cm)
Bequest of Musa Guston, 1992

RACHEL HARRISON   American, b. 1966
Huffy Howler   2004
wood, polystyrene, Parex, cement,
acrylic, Huffy Howler bicycle, various
black handbags, rocks, stones, gravel,
brick, sheep skin, long metal pole,
slightly enlarged publicity still of
Mel Gibson in Braveheart, binder clips
84 x 84 x 30 in.
(213.4 x 213.4 x 76.2 cm) installed
T. B. Walker Acquisition Fund, 2008

Al Gore   2007
wood, chicken wire, polystyrene,
Parex, cement, acrylic, Honeywell T87
thermostat
85 x 34 x 17 in.
(215.9 x 86.4 x 43.2 cm)
Courtesy the artist and Greene Naftali,
New York

Chicken   2008
wood pedestal, acrylic, photograph,
rubber toy chicken, sawdust
44 x 70 x 22 in.
(111.8 x 177.8 x 55.9 cm)
Private collection
Courtesy the artist, Meyer Kainer
Galerie, Vienna and Greene Naftali,
New York

THOMAS HIRSCHHORN   Swiss, b. 1957
Untitled   1992
plastic, foil, adhesive tape,
magazine prints on paper
53½ x 85½ in.
(135.9 x 217.2 cm) installed
T. B. Walker Acquisition Fund, 2007

Abstract Resistance   2006
cardboard, paint, wood, tape, chains,
carpet, cloth banner, screws, nails,
electrical wire, printed materials,
television monitors, DVD players,
florescent-light fixtures, wooden beams
with text of nails, wood logs, hammers,
drills, plastic bucket
192 x 275 x 129 in.
(487.7 x 698.5 x 327.7 cm) installed
T. B. Walker Acquisition Fund, 2006

ELLSWORTH KELLY   American, b. 1923
Ground Zero   2003
collage on paper
11⁹⁄₁₆ x 13½ in.
(29.4 x 34.3 cm) irregular
Whitney Museum of American Art, New York
Gift of an anonymous donor

PAUL MCCARTHY   American, b. 1945
Black and White Tapes   1970–1975/1993
videotape (black and white, sound);
32:50 minutes
T. B. Walker Acquisition Fund, 2002

ROBERT MOTHERWELL   American, 1915–1991
Histoire d'un Peintre
(Diary of a Painter)   1956
crayon, paper on rag board
16 x 12 in.
(40.6 x 30.5 cm)
Gift of Margaret and Angus Wurtele and
the Dedalus Foundation, 1995

BRUCE NAUMAN   American, b. 1941
Poke in the Eye/Nose/Ear 3/8/94 Edit
1994
video projector, videodisc player,
videodisc (color, silent); 52 minutes
T. B. Walker Acquisition Fund, 1994

CADY NOLAND   American, b. 1956
Untitled   2008
metal basket, motorcycle helmets, film
reel, subway straps, cast-metal object
13½ x 25½ x 13¼ in.
(34.3 x 64.8 x 33.7 cm)
Gift of the artist and Helen van der
Meij-Tcheng by exchange, 2009

CHARLES RAY   American, b. 1953
Unpainted Sculpture   1997
fiberglass, paint
60 x 78 x 171 in.
(152.4 x 198.1 x 434.3 cm)
Gift of Bruce and Martha Atwater, Ann
and Barrie Birks, Dolly Fiterman, Erwin
and Miriam Kelen, Larry Perlman and
Linda Peterson Perlman, Harriet and
Edson Spencer with additional funds from
the T. B. Walker Acquisition Fund, 1998

GEDI SIBONY   American, b. 1973
Not Too Different   2006
carpet
87 x 72½ in.
(221 x 184.2 cm)
Justin Smith Purchase Fund, Butler
Family Fund, Julie and Babe Davis
Acquisition Fund, 2007

Than   2006–2007
enamel spray paint
36½ x 35½ in. (92.7 x 90.2 cm)
Justin Smith Purchase Fund, Butler
Family Fund, Julie and Babe Davis
Acquisition Fund, 2007

Shhhh   2007
corrugated cardboard, adhesive tape,
video monitor/player, videotape
(black and white, silent); continuous
96 x 48 x 36 in.
(243.8 x 121.9 x 91.4 cm)
Justin Smith Purchase Fund, Butler
Family Fund, Julie and Babe Davis
Acquisition Fund, 2007

So   2007
plexiglass
42⅞ x 42⅜ x 3½ in.
(108.9 x 107.6 x 8.9 cm)
Justin Smith Purchase Fund, Butler
Family Fund, Julie and Babe Davis
Acquisition Fund, 2007

The World In Its Mouth   2007
pegboard
64⅞ x 42½ in.
(164.8 x 108 cm) inner sheet;
96½ x 48⅛ in.
(245.1 x 122.2 cm) outer sheet
Justin Smith Purchase Fund, Butler
Family Fund, Julie and Babe Davis
Acquisition Fund, 2007

KARA WALKER   American, b. 1969
Search for ideas supporting the Black
Man as a work of Modern Art/Contemporary
Painting. A death without end: an
appreciation of the Creative Spirit of
Lynch Mobs—   2007
ink on 52 sheets of paper
22½ x 28½ in.
(57.2 x 72.4 cm) each
T. B. Walker Acquisition Fund, 2009

ANDRO WEKUA   Georgian, b. 1977
Spectator Standing   2005
wax figure with clothing, oil,
velvet, foil, paper on canvas
80½ x 70⅞ x 29 in.
(204.5 x 180 x 73.7 cm)
T. B. Walker Acquisition Fund, 2006

CATHY WILKES   Northern Irish, b. 1967
Mummy's Here   2009
oil and tempera on canvas
14¹⁵⁄₁₆ x 18⅛ in.
(38 x 46 cm)
Private collection, Toby Webster,
Glasgow

Untitled   2009
oil and tempera on canvas
7¹⁄₁₆ x 9¹³⁄₁₆ in. (18 x 25 cm)
Collection HMT, Berlin

Galilee   2009–2010
mixed media
dimensions variable
Courtesy the artist, Galerie Giti
Nourbakhsch, Berlin, and The Modern
Institute/Toby Webster Ltd, Glasgow

Selected Bibliography

Adorno, Theodor W. Negative Dialectic. New York: Continuum, 2007.

Baudrillard, Jean. Simulations. New York: Semiotext(e), 1983.

Butler, Judith. Giving an Account of Oneself. New York: Fordham University Press, 2005.

De Zegher, Catherine. 3 x Abstraction: New Methods of Drawing: Hilma af Klint, Emma Kunz, Agnes Martin. New York: Drawing Center, 2005.

Droschl, Sandro, and Norbert Pfaffenbichler. Abstraction Now. Vienna: Künstlerhaus, 2003.

Dziewior, Yilmaz. Formalism: Modern Art, Today. Hamburg, Germany: Kunstverein Hamburg, 2004.

Ellegood, Anne. The Uncertainty of Objects and Ideas: Recent Sculpture. Washington, D.C.: Hirschhorn Museum and Sculpture Garden, 2006.

Fer, Brioney. On Abstract Art. New Haven, Conn.: Yale University Press, 1997.

Flood, Richard, Massimiliano Gioni, and Laura Hoptman. Unmonumental: Falling to Pieces in the 21st Century. New York: New Museum, 2007.

Foucault, Michel. Essential Works of Foucault, 1954–1984, vol. 3, Power. Edited by James D. Faubion. New York: New Press, 2000.

Garrels, Gary. Oranges and Sardines. Los Angeles: Hammer Museum, 2008.

Guston, Philip. Poem-Pictures. Andover, Mass.: Addison Gallery of American Art, 1994.

Jenkins, Bruce, and Susan Krane. Hollis Frampton: Recollection/ Recreations. Cambridge, Mass.: MIT Press, 1984.

Jones, Kellie, and Lowery Stokes Sims. Energy-Experimentation: Black Artists and Abstraction, 1964–1980. New York: Studio Harlem Museum, 2006.

Lotringer, Sylvère, and Paul Virilio. The Accident of Art. New York: Semiotext(e), 2005.

Lubiak, Jarosław. The Power of Formalism. Łódź, Poland: Muzeum Sztuki, 2007.

Madesta Andreas. Abstrakt/Abstract. Klagenfurt, Austria: Museum Moderner Kunst Karnten, 2008.

Marcoci, Roxana. Comic Abstraction: Image breaking, Image Making. New York: Museum of Modern Art, 2007.

Molesworth, Helen. Part Object Part Sculpture. Columbus, Ohio: Wexner Center for the Arts, 2005.

Pasolini, Pier Paolo. Roman Poems. San Francisco: City Lights, 2005.

Porter, Jenelle. Gone Formalism. Philadelphia: Institute of Contemporary Art, 2006.

Ranciere, Jacques. The Ignorant School-master: Five Lesson in Intellectual Emancipation. Stanford, California: Stanford University Press, 1991.

Lenders to the Exhibition

Anthology Film Archives, New York
Collection HMT, Berlin
Galerie Giti Nourbakhsch, Berlin
Gallery Meyer Kainer, Vienna
Greene Naftali Gallery, New York
The Modern Institute/Toby Webster Ltd., Glasgow
Toby Webster, Glasgow
Walker Art Center, Minneapolis
Whitney Museum of American Art, New York

Contributors

SIMON BAIER, an art historian and critic, is a research fellow at the NCCR Iconic Criticism, University of Basel, Switzerland. He is a PhD candidate in art history at the University of Basel, with a focus on theory of installation in 20th-century art. Baier has contributed to publications by the artist collectives Continuous Project and Scorched Earth as well as Spike Art Quarterly and Texte zur Kunst. He is a graduate of the Independent Study Program of the Whitney Museum of American Art, New York.

THOMAS HIRSCHHORN is a Paris-based Swiss artist known for working with an expanded idea of sculpture that operates in a variety of social spaces, including the gallery, the museum, the street, or specific urban communities. His work has been shown at major international venues, including Galerie Crousel, Centre Georges Pompidou, and Palais de Tokyo, Paris; Tate Modern, London; Gladstone Gallery, New York; Institute of Contemporary Art, Boston; Walker Art Center, Minneapolis; Museo Tamayo Arte Contemporáneo, Mexico; 2006 Bienal de São Paulo, Brazil; Documenta XI, Kassel, Germany; and the 48th Venice Biennale.

YASMIL RAYMOND is a curator at Dia Art Foundation, New York. Formerly she was an associate curator at the Walker Art Center, Minneapolis (2004–2009), where she organized exhibitions of works by Tomás Saraceno, Tino Sehgal and Kara Walker (with Philippe Vergne); and the group exhibitions Statements: Beuys, Flavin, Judd and Brave New Worlds (with Doryun Chong). She has written texts on Mircea Cantor, Cao Fei, Iñigo Manglano-Ovalle, Rivane Neuenschwander, Todd Norsten, Kiki Smith, and Haegue Yang. She received a BFA from the School of the Art Institute of Chicago (1999), and an MA from the Center for Curatorial Studies at Bard College (2004).

GEDI SIBONY, a New York–based artist, has been featured in solo exhibitions at venues such as the Contemporary Art Museum, St. Louis; Greene Naftali Gallery, New York; Midway Contemporary Art, Minneapolis; Galerie Art : Concept, Paris; and the Wrong Gallery, New York. His recent group exhibitions include Now You See It, Aspen Art Museum, Colorado; Genesis I'm Sorry, Greene Naftali, New York; Unmonumental, New Museum of Contemporary Art, New York; and the 2006 Whitney Biennial, Whitney Museum of Art, New York. He received an MFA from Columbia University, New York (2000).

MARCUS STEINWEG is a Berlin-based philosopher and writer. His recent publications include Aporien der Liebe (2010), Duras (2008), Behauptungsphilosophie (2006), Subjektsingularitäten (2004), and Bataille Maschine (2003). Steinweg regularly collaborates with artist Thomas Hirschhorn on his large-scale politically inspired projects and publications, including Spinoza-Map; The Map of Friendship between Art and Philosophy; and Utopia Utopia = One World, One War, One Army, One Dress, co-organized by the Institute of Contemporary Art, Boston, and Wattis Institute, San Francisco.

CATHY WILKES is a Glasgow-based artist whose solo exhibitions include the Modern Institute, Transmission Gallery, Glasgow; Cubitt Gallery, London; Migros Museum, Zurich; Douglas Hyde Gallery, Dublin; Galerie Giti Nourbakhsch, Berlin; and Milton Keynes Gallery, United Kingdom. Her many group exhibitions include Beck's Futures, ICA, London; 4th Gwangju Biennial, South Korea; Independence, South London Gallery; Selective Memory, Scottish Pavilion, Venice Biennale, and Scottish National Gallery of Modern Art, Edinburgh; 4th Berlin Biennial for Contemporary Art; and If I Can't Dance, I Don't Want To Be Part Of Your Revolution, MuHKA Museum van Hedendaagse Kunst, Antwerp. Wilkes completed her studies at the Glasgow School of Art and the University of Ulster, Belfast.

Photography Credits

All images are installation views of the exhibition Abstract Resistance at the Walker Art Center, Minneapolis. Specific artworks are identified below by page number. Photos: Gene Pittman, Walker Art Center

7   left: CHARLES RAY
Unpainted Sculpture 1997

foreground (right): ANTHONY CARO
Sculpture Three, 1962 1962
(detail)

8-9   foreground: ANTHONY CARO
Sculpture Three, 1962 1962

right (on wall): LUCIO FONTANA
Concetto Spaziale-Attesa
(Spatial Concept-Expectation)
1958

10   LYNDA BENGLIS
Element from Adhesive Products
1971 (detail)

11   CHARLES RAY
Unpainted Sculpture 1997 (detail)

12-13 Installation view of Gallery 4

14   ANDRO WEKUA
Spectator Standing 2005

49   foreground: BRUCE CONNER
THE BRIDE 1960

50-51 foreground (left): RACHEL HARRISON
Al Gore 2007

center: RACHEL HARRISON
Chicken 2008

right (on wall): SARAH CHARLESWORTH
April 21, 1978 from Modern History
1978 (detail)

52   RACHEL HARRISON
Al Gore 2007 (detail)

53   PHILIP GUSTON
Bombay 1976 (detail)

54-55 left (on wall): THOMAS HIRSCHHORN
Untitled 1992

center left (on wall): PHILIP GUSTON
Bombay 1976

center: THOMAS HIRSCHHORN
Abstract Resistance 2006 (detail)

right (on wall): HOLLIS FRAMPTON
Untitled I-XIV from ADSVMVS
ABSVMVS 1982 (detail)

56-57 foreground (left):
RACHEL HARRISON
Huffy Howler 2004

center: ELLSWORTH KELLY
Ground Zero 2003

right (on wall): HOLLIS FRAMPTON
Untitled I-XIV from ADSVMVS
ABSVMVS 1982 (detail)

58   THOMAS HIRSCHHORN
Abstract Resistance 2006 (detail)

80-81 foreground (right): CATHY WILKES
Galilee 2009-2010

left (on wall): KARA WALKER
Search for ideas supporting the
Black Man as a work of Modern Art/
Contemporary Painting. A death
without end: an appreciation of
the Creative Spirit of Lynch Mobs—
2007 (detail)

center (on wall): FRANCIS BACON
Head in Gray 1955

82,83 CATHY WILKES
Galilee 2009-2010 (details)

84-85 foreground (left): CATHY WILKES
Galilee 2009-2010

left (on wall, from left to
right): CATHY WILKES
Mummy's Here and Untitled 2009

right: BRUCE NAUMAN
Poke in the Eye/Nose/Ear 3/8/94
Edit 1994

86-87 foreground (left): GEDI SIBONY
Shhhh 2007

center: GEDI SIBONY
The World In Its Mouth 2007

right: GEDI SIBONY
Not Too Different 2006

88   CATHY WILKES
Galilee 2009-2010 (detail)

Walker Postscript—the Walker Art Center's new print-on-demand publishing imprint—presents short and focused texts that delve more deeply, or broadly, into the rich concepts that animate the institution's diverse artistic programs.

www.ingramcontent.com/pod-product-compliance
Lightning Source LLC
Chambersburg PA
CBHW030909180526
45163CB00004B/1765